Dancing Room Only

Other Books by Jim Reese

Poetry

These Trespasses (Backwaters Press, 2005)

ghost on 3rd (NYQ Books,, 2010)

Really Happy! (NYQ Books, 2014)

Nonfiction

Bone Chalk (Stephen F. Austin State Unitveristy Press, 2020)

Dancing Room Only

New and Selected Poems

by

Jim Reese

The New York Quarterly Foundation, Inc.
Beacon, New York

NYQ Books™ is an imprint of The New York Quarterly Foundation, Inc.

The New York Quarterly Foundation, Inc.
P. O. Box 470
Beacon, NY 12508

www.nyq.org

First Edition

Set in New Baskerville

Layout by Raymond P. Hammond

Cover Art: "GeezySS" by Bret Gottschal

Author Photograph by Saralyn D Photography

Library of Congress Control Number: 2023932993

ISBN: 978-1-63045-073-1

for

Maria Mazzioti Gillan & Ray Hammond

Contents

ghost on 3rd (NYQ Books, 2010)

Dancing Room Only (NYQ Books, 2023)

Acknowledgements

Thanks to Greg Kosmicki and The Backwaters Press for permission to reprint poems from my first book, *These Trespasses*. Grateful acknowledgments to the following publications and their editors in which most of these poems first appeared in one form or another: *4 P.M. Count, The Backwaters Press, Benedictines, Caduceus—the Journal for the Physicians of Yale University, Cairn, Saint Andrews Press, Clover—A Literary Rag, Connecticut Review, Connecticut River Review, Harpur Palate, Lips, Little Patuxent Review, Louisiana Literature Review, Mid-America Poetry Review, Midwest Quarterly, MiPOesias, Nebraska Life, New York Quarterly, NYQ Books, Oakwood, Pasqual Petals, Paterson Literary Review, Phoenix in the Jacuzzi Journal, Platte Valley Review, Poetry East, PoetryMagazine.com, poetsandartists.com, Prairie Schooner, Plain Song Review, South Dakota Magazine, South Dakota Review, Talking River Review, Touchstone.*

Some of these poems have been reprinted in the following anthologies, broadsides/animated storyboards: Nebraska Presence: The State of Poetry, *The Backwaters Press*, Watching the Perseids—*The Backwaters Press* Twentieth Anniversary Anthology, The Harvest of Words: Contemporary South Dakota Poetry, *Center for Western Studies*, Down the Brown River, *Louisiana Literature Press*, The American Voice in Poetry: the Legacy of Whitman, Williams, and Ginsberg *Paterson Literary Review/ Poetry Center Paterson, New Jersey*, Survive and Thrive: Starts with the Heart, ed. Rex Veeder, Words Like Rain, *WSC Press*. "The Keeper of All Things Whole and Necessary," 2013, words by Jim Reese, drawing by Alice Leora Briggs, all rights reserved. "Triple Dog Dares" Poster Design by Young Ae Kim for the P3 Invitational Exhibition of paired poems and artwork—Washington Pavilion of Arts and Science, Sioux Falls, SD, 2008. "Willing and Ready" 100 copies printed on letterpress by Fine Arts Press, University of Nebraska-Omaha, 2006.

Thank you to Raymond Hammond and NYQ Books for the years of faith in my work and for believing in me! Kent Meyers, Mike Reese, Jamie Sullivan, Stephanie Schultz, Marielle Frigge and Neil Harrison for their time, patience, steadfast and caring criticism. Maria Mazziotti Gillan—for your *Inimitable Heart* and giving a young poet a chance to travel east and perform when no other editor would. The Lammers and Reese family for their love, patience and letting me tell my stories. Thanks to Marc Long and Mount Marty University for a sabbatical which allowed me time to write and finish this book. Joe Weil, George Bilgere, Ted Kooser, Jim Daniels, Kevin Clark, David Lee, Don Welch, Bill Kloefkorn, JV Brummels, Barbara Schmitz, Chuck Bowden, Bret Gottschall, Vivian Shipley, Dave Pichaske, Daryl Farmer, Jonis Agee, Patrick Hicks, Fran Streff, Christine Stewart, Jon Lauck, Marilyn Johnson, James Engelhardt, Daniel Flahie, Stephen Bell, Jason Heron, Lynn Golodner, Nathan Johnson, Dan Jenkins, Josh Klimek, Jerold Ryken, Ross Den Herder, Dave "His poetry doesn't even rhyme!" Dannenbring, and Javy Murguia. To my past and present students at Mount Marty and at the prisons where I teach—thanks for always pushing me to practice what I preach. And of course for Linda, Willow and Paige—for letting me recite poetry out loud at the dinner table every night. Abrazos.

Dancing Room Only

These Trespasses (The Backwaters Press, 2005)

Ten Penny High

Friday nights at Vernon's place
Felice, feeling loose,
unbuttoning clothes.
We chisel ice for our drinks
out of an old plastic ice-cream tub
long gone of vanilla and chocolate swirl.
The summer heat unbearable,
ice picks and iron fans,
humidity and cling.

Sitting on one of the kitchen's mismatched chairs
Felice spreads her legs wide
and begins icing her cleavage and lips.
Vernon turns on the record player,
starts spinning forty-fives.
Felice grabs us one after another,
leads us in dance.

I got songs to bring it up,
and songs to take it down, Vernon hollers.
And don't be taking advantage of my wife,
you hear?

Before long Vernon drifts off
somewhere else, sometimes physically,
looking for what he calls his
Ten penny high.

Some sugar is right through
that bedroom door, Felice whispers,
tonguing an ear.
That's our cue to leave.

We all think about it on the way home.
Some of us talk about it,
some of us joke about it,
some of us, sitting in the back seat,
don't say a word.

707 Florence Boulevard

"Coltrane on the stereo, pushing up the volume
once again." — *Drive-By-Honky*

Where we used to go
buy beer back in high school.
Just went to the corner liquor store
until Vernon got smart and made us
pick him up at his apartment.
Always had to have an extra five dollars
for his fifth of Skol.

The apartment, with its flaking
light blue walls, smelled like a sweaty ass.
We wouldn't sit on the couch
but sometimes passed out on it.
We stayed, always too long.

There was no art on the walls,
just his daughter's honor roll certificates,
and in the corner a turntable spinning 45s.
We ate gizzards there. We drank and sang.
We danced with Vernon's wife,
until she talked dirty to us.

The night she asked Chuck
to feel her up, and he didn't—
the night she stabbed
Vernon in the stomach
because he couldn't get it up—
was the last time we bought beer
on a regular basis.

Strike On the Stoop

When Vernon said to hell with it
and decided not to stand in line
at the corner to see if he could
get himself some work, you knew it
was going to be one of those days.

Solly, wearing his girlfriend's bikini
briefs and two different socks, came out
on the stoop to see for himself.
If you ain't going, I ain't either.

Clarence,
who hadn't gone down
to the corner the last month and a half,
came out, yawned, dug his hand
in his shorts and scratched himself.

They all sat, watched the bus go by,
watched kids go to and from school.
They saw the street sweeper
pass by twice, and called it a day.

Vernon's Unenjoyment Check

Supposedly Vernon's monthly unemployment
check was cut on the third of every month
and in the mail from the state that day.
On the fourth or fifth of each month
he'd come and wait down on the stoop
for Fred the mailman to deliver the goods.
Fred came every day but Tuesday.
That was his day off.

Vernon always had a string of debt
from the prior month's sour offerings.
Everybody always wantin' something, he'd say.
*Man's always taking, Felice wants perfume,
and I gotta find me a trumpet for my daughter.
Hell, we all got to eat. Gotta get my forty, too.*

By the sixth day, Vernon, skinny as grade school
toilet paper, would be bumming smokes
and living off everyone else's dole.
He'd start getting itchy and agitated,
looking down, scratching at the backs of his hands.

Maybe the man cut you off, Vernon.
Someone always said it.

God damn. I'm disabled. Can't get cut.

Disabled. Where?

And it went on like this until Fred
The Working Man came with the check
and Vernon bought everyone forties and smokes
and did his monthly dance on the front stoop.

Just call me the bird, he'd say,
as he boogied barefoot into the night.

20

At the Bar with Bella

Give me a shot of Cuervo
with training wheels, she said.
And fill this guy up.
That's all it took. She had me.
I watched her hammer one back
and then another. She sucked
on the limes, tore them to rind,
ordered a bloody beer,
slid onto the stool next to me.
Wedding cake and funeral ham
are my two favorite kinds of food.
I'm serious, she said.
Think about it.
I did. She made all the sense
in the world.

Prenuptial Retreat

It was a Sunday afternoon.
Overcast. We sat in
the Catholic Retreat Center,
doodling on our clipboards,
adding our own engravings
next to those of others who had come
before us—next to
Jake loves Michelle forever!
and
This place sucks,
I'd rather be in hell.

That Sunday we sat
and listened to a priest question
his faith and life choices.
How he still remembered his high school
sweetheart, how he'd experienced
some himself, and how he'd sinned
and repented. How he wondered what
she might be doing now.

We paid two-hundred dollars
to swap quiz bowl questions
about each other's feelings
and watch a wide-eyed natural planner
talk to us about creating babies, and his swing set,
and the odd days of the month.

* * *

I do believe
we are all created equal,
just some screwed together a little
looser or tighter
than the others.

I do believe
that it's a good idea to own a dog
before you raise
a child of your own.

I think everyone, at least once,
should ride shotgun in a loaded
grain truck with spotty brakes.
I believe it might slow people
down a bit.

I do believe,
but have my questions.

I do believe that priest
should get on a bus,
find his high school sweetheart.

For better or worse,
I do.

At the Track with Pauline

Sundays after the almighty sermon
and brunch, when the rest of the family
thinks I'm taking her home for a nap,
my grandma and I hammer the car
to Prairie Meadows. She likes watching
the jockeys walk on soft dirt between
stables, keeping them at eye level.

When the heat and fever grow unbearable
we drop a three-dollar bet on the same
trifecta grouping, 1-2-3.
When the unofficial results
say different, we head to the slots
for the progressive jackpot.

We each have our own ritual.
I take my time inserting quarters
and pulling the handle.
She feeds the machine with dollars
and crosses her heart with each new
greenback. The days we get to winning
and drinking 50-cent Chablis,
when the diamonds do repetitive rolls
and the jokers align, it truly is
heaven right here in Iowa.

Morse Code

Donnie Kleats says it himself:
I'm an old mean sonofagun,
my pension pissed down the toilet
and I'm still waiting for money
from the government so I can
retire in style.

After his call of duty he worked
45 years as a plate setter
for the *Daily Tribune,* and nothing
to show for it now except a free
subscription to what he calls
the piss-poor paper.

Kleats fought overseas.
Killed men he was programmed to
eliminate. Got his Morse code tooth pulled out,
he says, the one that took him on
secret missions. No proof now
that he was in a godforsaken war.

Verla pours him red beers at the
Air Force Base bar. He says he'd get a
Tap Tap Tap coming by satellite
on his back right molar.
They came in 15 second intervals, he says.
*Codes were given and instructions followed
on the nearest land phone. Can you
imagine having a goddamn telegram
going off in your mouth for 40 years?*

He turns to me,
*Well, I can, you little turd. No one
believes a word I say. Ask Verla
if you don't believe me. More than once
her and I have been in the middle*

of churning our own butter when
my mouth started vibrating.

It's always the same static. The exact
details that keep me intrigued and
an ear bent in his direction.
And when the jets come in low for a
landing and the barroom walls start
to shake, I watch him grind his teeth
and roll his eyes directionless
until he deadpans on Verla.
Sitting and waiting, I suppose,
for his next *Tap Tap Tap*
to come in.

Calendars

Here at work at the halfway house we receive free calendars from the local pharmacy in town. Every holiday season they send us ten for free with a thank-you card for another year of good business. They give these away to all their customers advertising their pharmaceutical wares. At the bottom of each month I read the pharmacy name, location and its number for business. I call that number every once in a while to see if next year's calendars are in yet. Depicted on the top of each month are scenes—a little girl learning to ride her bike, a grandfather teaching his grandson how to fish, and so on. Written on the back of the calendar are pertinent farming and gardening tips and the projected sunrises and sunsets of various days. I exploit the calendar for the whole year. Then I cut the pictures out, frame them, and give them to my relatives for Christmas.

Nebraska Bumper Stickers (Circa 2005)

Don't be shy, show me some thigh as you pass by

Cowboy Butts Drive Me Nuts

If you can read this the **BITCH** fell off

Don't let the car fool you, my treasure is in heaven

A cartoon Alvin peeing—Piss On Ex-Wife
Piss On Ford
Piss On It
Piss on Bush—all on the same truck

I Want To Be Like Barbie, *That Bitch Has Everything*

GO SKERS!

Eat Pork, the other White Meat

No Farmers, No Future

EAT BEEF it's GOOD FOR YA'

Don't tailgate me; I'll flick a booger on your windshield

Demo Drivers Bong Harder

Picasso Trigger Sodomized My Honor Roll Student

Keep Your Politics Off My Ovaries

BUCK FUSH!

Support Our Troops

Ask Me about Mary Kay

Honk If You're On **Lithium**!

YEAH GOD!

Books Are Heavy

My Sister Is In the Air Force

Abolish the Death Penalty

HAGFISH Rocks Your Lame Ass

I Got Mine at Tooties,
Hartington, NE

The Dam Bait Shop—Our Minnows Will Catch Fish or Die Trying

It's All about the Rack

American Chicken Haulers Association

Flirt Harder, I'm a Physicist

Another Christian Against the Christian Coalition

At Least I Can Still Smoke In My Car

He's Not My President

Baby Cowgirl on Board

FOCUS ON YOUR OWN DAMN FAMILY

"AMERICA, BEND OVER!"

Phil's Pizza and Porn Deliveries

My Other Wife is a **Hummer**

Talk to ME *Not My TITS*

This Vehicle Stops at ALL DOG Shows

GO HUSKERS!!!

3 Nails + 1 Cross = 4GVN

Thespians DO IT on Stage

On A Quiet Day You Can Hear A Ford Rusting

How Many Cowboys Does It Take To Open A Beer?
None. It Should Be Open When She Brings It To You.

CANCER SUCKS

I Mucked 30 Stalls Before 8:00 a.m.
What Did You Do?

Euchre at Two

Picture Main Street. A bar full of farmers
sitting at round tables, clean overalls.
The stench of stale beer and urinals run dry.
Hear fists slamming down on oak, the louder
the better hand. See Ernest and Linus,
57-year-old identical twins,
pause between bites of pie to see for themselves.

Imagine a more serious affair
than prices dropping $3.00 a bushel—
banker pockets swelling with sweet deals while
every decent man's job runs awry.
Hear Edsel holler, *More money
in selling the kernel to Hy-Vee for lawn
ornaments and deecor than giving her away!*

Loose change slides impatiently from one pocket
to another. Like ghost feathers, there's a muffled
Open. In. Come on.
Squinting lids, shifting pupils, and wide eyes
show all their white. Hands hold five bid,
no bid, Busch Light.

Fist banging against table,
table on top of floor,
floor covering foundation
over this land they pound.

Willing and Ready

1870 – 1933. Floyd R. Knipplemeyer, Farmer. Will concluded on said date of December 13th 1930, Cedar County, Nebraska:

To son Floyd Jr., 80 acres of broke ground of his choosing—quarter horses and the 30 aught 6. East side of house. All out buildings.

Son Ronald T. 87 Head of Angus. West side of house. North forty. Outhouse squatting rights.

Daughter Florence. 1 Hereford Bull. Mother's wedding ring to do with as you choose. All household appliances, furniture and accessories except, Ronald T. and Floyd Junior's beds, kitchen table and wood stove. Said savings of $16,328 and 33 cents.

Neighbor. Floyd Sr. grants permission to finally move fence at the south end of Snake Creek. You're welcome you son of a bitch.

Witness. Mary A. Armkanecht. Dec. 13th 1933.

Ritual

Harold Cummins never learned to drive.
Says he never had anywhere worth going.
He's a 69-year-old German farmer
who fought in the Korean War.
He's lived in the big house his grandfather
built since he was born. Only gone once for
that call of duty in Pusan, never married.

The rides he does get are to and from church
every Saturday night, and to a handful
of family get-togethers.
You know, they were saying...
Well, he gets that information from the
Yankton Press and Dakotan.
One summer I watched him cut up
an old washer and dryer using tin snips—
into three-inch squares.

Mornings, you can see him through the kitchen
window, thumbing the paper, and again at noon.
In between meals and chores he sits on a
feeder bucket, head over a rusted coffee can,
where he breaks up glass bottles.

In a rhythmic movement, he quarter-turns
an old rusted ball hitch, grinding the bottles
into fine sand. When the can is full,
he takes the bottles' remains and spreads them
down the lane, creating his own glass highway.

Last fall he'd made a trail with the sand
a quarter mile up the lane before
that first winter blow. If he lived somewhere
warmer, where the trail might grow all the way
to the road, I wonder which way he'd go?

Homegrown

Peculiar and quiet, from a broken home,
George spent summer afternoons watching me
tear down what was left of a fallen barn
to make room for another enormous garden
his foster parents wouldn't share with anyone.

George helped me pick up the pieces by hand,
held salvageable two-by-sixes on
sawhorses as I hammered out every
last rusted nail. Almost every afternoon
he did this. Then he'd be gone for days.

The curtains would be pulled at the place,
the sound of piano keys, redundant
chord progressions and John Thompson techniques
echoing in the air. On those days
I thought it was wrong. George not around,
cooped up in that stuffy house, forced into
some sort of homegrown recital.

* * *

When the barn was done and I returned to
graduate school I forgot about George.

Two years later on the local news
I saw a picture of the house,
the two gardens gone to weeds,
and a newscaster reporting that
the foster parents were accused of tying
a child to his bed and feeding him homegrown
habanero peppers.

All this education, I think,
and I never stopped once to ask George,
Is everything okay?

34

Animals

There are thirty-seven stuffed animals
mounted on these walls. Five-by-fives and buckskin
over beer taps and booze. There are roosters
on the run. Two wide-eyed coyotes stopped
in mid-dance, a full-breasted turkey
fanning itself. There's a large shadow box
full of forty pounds of Missouri catfish
hooked on a stringer and polished with
polyurethane. Leaning on the bar
and swiveling on round stools are men in
camouflage and Carhartt coveralls,
all of them immortalized among
wildlife and fowl. It's been dark outside
for hours, but in here life illuminates.

Hear the cackle and howl carry down
Main Street, echoing call after call.
Listen as Harold Tahatchenbach,
blinder than a raccoon in headlights,
bends the truth. Everyone knows he likely
put more bullets in the sky today
than the lot of us. See Linus Cummins
prance around with antlers on his head.
This year's trophy a suck'n buck
proudly worn for all to see.
Jeremiah Knipplemeyer,
with one eye cocked, will sit at the corner
of the bar regurgitating
how he let that one get away.
All these bullets and BB's, beers and bowls.
All this bullshitting, for big game,
bragging rights and blast.

The Paperboy

—for Dave Lee

Now, over here the first thing you've got to do
is tie these here like this, on both sides.
Otherwise the papers will
come loose, and you'll lose them,
and they won't stand for that at the Post.

This tie-er is tricky.
You've gotta play with her.
Hell, give her a name if you want.
Last fella called her Betty. Said it
worked better for him that way.
Anyhow, if it gets tangled
you gotta go in with your hands
and pull it out. And if that don't work,
then you're gonna have to get some pliers.
And trust me, you'll need 'em.
I got a pair you can use for today,
but come tomorrow, you better
have your own.

See. Rips right out like this.
She's just a bitch to re-string is all,
and there's no time to reload her
when the papers come pouring in.
Okay, now over here you got your bags.
Hook 'em here. It makes it easier
so you don't have to hassle
with throwing 'em in by hand.
Each bag's got a label too.
You got your Pilger Route, Pilger City,
here. You got your Hoskins, Randolph,
Crofton, and Wynot over here.
And you have to circle Wynot's.
Don't ask why—alls I know
is they'll send them back

and then you'll have to drive them
out there in the morning
and they'll already be late.
LaVerta Hughes—she'll bitch
because she didn't read it first-hand.
And all it really is, is a circle.
So don't forget!

Your Hartington and Laurel go over
here. Same with Ponca.
Don't forget to circle them, too.
If you think it needs a circle,
circle it. Hell, circle them all
for all I care. Otherwise, they'll
send them back like the pigs in Wynot.
Bastards can't figure out to just look
if it ain't labeled right.

All the ones from Wayne go on this cart.
And listen here very carefully,
they're priority number one.
They have to be at the post office by six o'clock.
They like them earlier, but six is the latest.
Any later and they'll leave without 'em,
and then you're fucked.
Wouldn't even come back to work
if that happens.
When you drop off the papers
you have to give them this envelope,
otherwise it's not authorized.
They want their money first of course.
Close them all up tight.
Load 'em—Wayne on this side
and the others on the other side.
That way, you can differentiate.

No smoking in the truck either.
In case of some accident we only got
liability, so be careful.
This truck will get you there if you got faith
in the Lord, but the Lord
didn't get the spare fixed yet,
so watch out for them potholes.

Premeditation

I'm watching my daughter sleep,
her eyes dancing under the heavy lids
of dream. I can only hope that I'll
do my part the best way I know how.
In this family there must be no question of love.

> He did it. We all know he did it.
> A seventeen-year-old convicted felon.
> I also know his father was serving
> time in prison. What kind of father was he?
>
> In high school hallways people whispered
> about his whereabouts while the news
> flashed his picture over and over and over.
> Phone lines were cut. A letter was written.
> The child was corralled by an accomplice
> while he bound Christine, the babysitter,
> my friend, and raped, tortured and killed her.

I watch my daughter dreaming,
and when she wakes I pick her up.
I know I can't go through life fearing
what I can't foresee. I will not ruin
myself thinking this way.

Her eyes are open.
I am holding on—
tight.

Leftovers

Friday for supper she prepared a tender roast
with all the fixings. Beef, potatoes, gravy,
onions, carrots and corn. We mashed the potatoes
with our forks. Sopped up the leftover gravy
on our plates with white bread.

On Saturday, for dinner, we had roast again.
Does it always taste better the next day?
Beef, potatoes, corn, more bread. Someone
sliced a tomato. Two of us shared a few
spoonfuls of gravy. That night, for supper,
we had it one more time. The beef and what was left
of the bread, mashed potatoes with butter
and a jar of applesauce. We chewed and chewed.

Sunday, thank the Almighty Lord,
we tackled the hock of a ham.

Wound Dresser

What stays with you latest and deepest? of curious panics,
of hard-fought engagements or sieges tremendous what
deepest remains?
                              —Walt Whitman

She is relieved from another night shift,
exhausted, with another story of dead flesh
from the burn unit—whole bodies decomposing
in front of her. I talk about you, Walt Whitman.
How you stayed year upon year dressing wounds,
dancing with soldiers, mending and tending
to the needs of your fellow man for free.
How you took in all the soldiers and their
blue and gray. She has your *Leaves* now, Walt.
She takes them with her each morning
to the deep end of the tub. I watch her hold on
as the black ink runs from the pages.
There will always be more editions
where that one came from.

On Calling about Walt Whitman's Brain

(1)
Welcome to the College of Physicians of Philadelphia. If you know your party's extension, press 1. For the Mutter Museum, press 2. The Mutter Museum hours are Monday through Sunday 10:00 a.m. to 5:00 p.m. Our Emerging Infectious Disease exhibit is now closed to make room for our compelling collection "Only One Man Died—Medical Adventures on the Lewis & Clark Trail." To leave a message for museum archives press 3.

(2)
Hi. I'm calling on behalf of research, our class project, inquiring about the poet Walt Whitman's brain. To our knowledge the brain may or may not be preserved at your facility. Rumor has it an assistant dropped the jar the encephalon had been stored in after it had been extracted, and we'd like to know if this assistant or others cleaned the contents up and might have put the brain in another jar, perhaps, and where they might have taken the remains—maybe, to your place. If that's the case, we'd like to venture on out and take a look at it. Can you give us a call if, in fact, we're contacting the right people, or let us know if we're just barking up the wrong tree.

(3)
Mr. Reese, Gretchen here from museum archives, returning your call into the inquiry of Walt Whitman's brain. Unfortunately, the brain is not here. The tissue and matter had been damaged beyond recognition when an assistant dropped the jar it was being preserved in. Hope that helps. If you have any further questions don't hesitate to call.

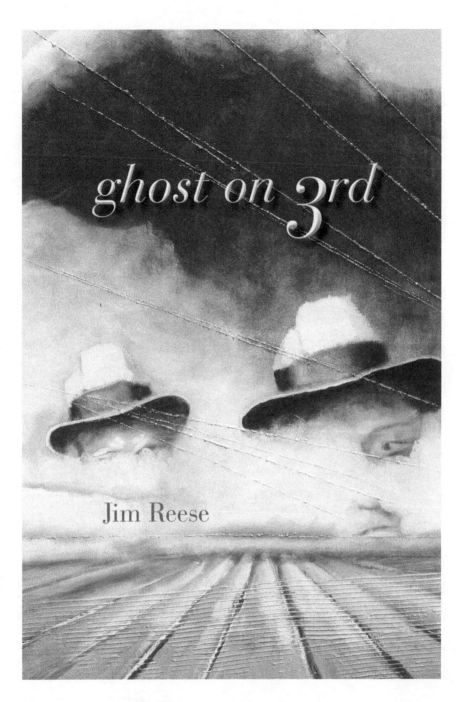

ghost on 3ʳᵈ (NYQ Books, 2010)

ghost on 3rd

At dusk, with my grandpa Cecil
and his soothsayer fishing buddy Russ,
I am on all fours hunting crawlers.
They hold flashlights and PBR's as
I wait with my tweezer-fingers to attack.

Don't let go, Junior, one says.
That's a keeper, all right.
I follow the light beams back and forth,
back and forth, attack, squeeze and pull
until the night crawler gives
or splits in two.

* * *

Grandpa, it's twenty-five years later
and I'm half a world away. You,
skinny as hospital tissue, lying
in a nursing home bed. Me, on my knees
crawling in garden rows searching for
crawlers, engulfed in dirt, bullsnake
and mosquitoes.

The last time we fished I had to ask for help
to lift you from the boat onto the dock,
bluegills and bass gone to grass carp
the size of Harleys.

This will never end. I will take the girls.
I will tell them about the fish hook
in my mother's head. How I saved you
from jumping overboard, how we hammered
fish for years.

Sleep, Grandpa, sleep.
You are the ghost on 3rd
and I'm sending you
home.

This Havelock

Possessive dandelions. Snot-nosed kids blowin' snowball-seeds into headwind. Then I come upon three plumber cracks bending over a '77 Vega, Old Milwaukee in each right hand, pocket-pool with each left. Fremont Street is full-blown with Harleys and homebrew, glass packs and malnourished mufflers. People driving. People bath-tub speeding. *Say, Sugar, you got somewhere to go or are you just going?* It's tube-tops and flip-flops, sidewalk stubbed toes, bare-knuckle, and third-shift swing. Arnold's Bar for orange breakfast beers, rocket fuel gin, a finger stir and Family Feud. Tobacco Shack porn and Misty's blackened prime—California Lunch Room brown bags and Bob's shuffle board. It's the Isles for hip-show tattoos and a Leaning Tower pie. It's rode hard and put away thirsty. 4 ½ amps on a hump day feeling a need for a need. I have to leave you, Havelock, this is my last stop. Stay here much longer, I won't make it to the week's end.

Jesus Christ Pose

I walk both sides of this fence.
I have no sympathy for those who
premeditate and execute heinous crimes.
In a theatre practicum in San Quentin
I watch you, a prisoner, standing
in the center of the room.

You raise your hands, palms up,
head dangling down, your Jesus Christ pose.
You begin to stand on one foot.
The room is quiet. People begin
shifting in their seats. Minutes pass.
You begin to lose your balance.
Every morning, you say, *after my foster
father left for work, she made me stand
in the corner like this.*

When your desperate left foot hits the ground
you scream in the voice of a child
being beaten. Now I understand why
some of you are here.

Coming to Grips

We are grilling at a friend's house. Watching
the game. Drinking a little beer, eating chips,
hotdogs, hamburgers—someone made artichoke dip.
You are running in the backyard, climbing
on patio furniture, chasing the dog.

Up and down and running. Up and down and running.
Chasing the dog. The other kids are playing
football. Babies, nursing. Your mother inside.
I can see her from where I'm sitting.
I catch a glimpse of you out of the corner
of my eye. You have climbed too high
on one of the plastic patio chairs, lost
your balance. And in one motion I am up,
arms outstretched, reaching, reaching.

I catch your shoulders inches before your head
hits the cement. You laugh. Don't know
how close you came. Your mother doesn't see
any of this. Some of the other parents
sigh. No one says anything. I am holding
on to you, tight.

We wave up to mom in the window.
She waves back. You say, *Wee!* Everyone
continues to play. Someone scores a touchdown.

I was at San Quentin and All I Got was This Lousy T-shirt

Pruno = Prison Wine

In the Sally Port as I leave the prison
I notice one of many signs hanging
on the old stone walls.

Don't forget to buy your
San Quentin T-shirt
TODAY ONLY.

I remember my colleague insisting,
Bring me back a souvenir and don't be
cheap about it.
In the parking lot overlooking the
San Francisco Bay, I inhale its salty
breeze. This 432 acres is prime
waterfront property. Even in this bust
market, real estate geeks believe
developers would pay $2 billion.

I approach the guard, the T-shirt vendor,
and like everything here, it's surreal.
There is a line. There are hoodies, various
apparel—all for sale. Proceeds to help
sustain San Quentin's Honor Guard Program.
I buy two identical T-shirts that
replicate a Jack Daniels bottle and read:

San Quentin Prison
Penn No. 1
1852
Cell-brewed
Pruno

So, I ask the guard, *You're selling T-shirts*
that promote a crime within the prison
to raise money for the Honor Guard?
Yeah.

Fair enough, I respond, as I turn and enter
a vehicle driven by an inmate
who will escort us off grounds. I flash him
the shirt and ask him if he wants one.

No way, man! I'm living this hell.

The Keeper of All Things Whole and Necessary

Puts leftover food in little plastic
baby food containers and yogurt cups
she has saved. Will leave half a chicken
wing for someone else to eat. Wraps up
and refrigerates one slice of bacon.
Puts lemon juice on half an apple
so it won't turn brown. Washes and saves
straws with holes and plastic silverware
with broken tines. Has a drawer full of mustard,
barbeque and soy sauce packages
from take-out restaurants.

Cuts coupons. Cuts up and collects newspaper
articles if she knows someone in the article
or knows someone who knows the person
in the article. Gives me play-by-plays
of garage sales and auctions. Saves fresh scraps
for stray cats—bones for the dogs. Saves for Jesus
and saves for you.

Picks green tomatoes before the first winter
freeze, wraps them in tissue paper and serves
them for Thanksgiving dinner. Balances
soap dispensers upside-down like others do
with ketchup bottles, and eventually
combines them in one bottle.

Has a room full of old jeans in case her husband's
overalls need patching or her son-in-law's
crotch blows out. Makes pie crust from hog lard.
(The only way to do it).
Has full canning jars from the 80's.
Has unidentifiable things older
than dirt in her deep freeze.

Once I saw her pull a tarp for a pick-up
bed out from underneath her dresser.
I've been holding on to this,
I don't know how long.

If you need something—a blow torch,
nunchucks, twist-ties, marbles,
propane, a chandelier, suspenders,
a curtain rod, spare tire,
a putter, basin wrench, bell bottoms,
                    a bowling ball—anything;
she's your woman.

As Seen on TV

The giant in first class is on flight 455 to Newark. The guy next to me in coach wonders if he's Andre the Giant. *No. He's dead,* the flight attendant says. *Giants only live so long because they grow so fast. Bone degeneration.* She looks at me and I say, *I'll have a giant vodka and orange juice.* I pick up the Sky Mall catalog and start to leaf through. A famous poet has said there are fifty of us on any given day in the air flying to and from readings. Today, only one poet on the same plane as a giant wrestler—I betcha. I'm tempted to concoct some sort of spit wad or non-identifiable object to throw at the back of the big guy's head, but the blue ruckus-reducing partition that divides us makes that nearly impossible. I don't want to piss him off. Just mess with him a little—get his attention, so I can ask him all those important questions. How big were your feet when you were born? How many boxes of macaroni and cheese can you eat before you come up for air? How fast could you kick this guy's ass next to me for blowing that spit wad at the back of your head? He'd have everyone's attention—after getting up, walking back to coach, hunkered over my row, each hand bigger than a headrest, eye-balling us.

Until I can make that happen, I have settled for this catalog—the indoor dog restroom and its antimicrobial porous turf—ideal for high-rise dwellings. Think gravity-defying boots and their patented T-spring system. An exhilarating low impact bounce—perfect for keeping tabs on the giant in your neighborhood. Interested in firm, sexy buns in two weeks? I am. The Shape and Form thingamajigger comes with unique toning pads that lift while you sit. When sporting your lifter why not wear your Flair Hair Visor. A built-in do and hat. And don't forget that portable 10" x 12" personal microwave—perfect for nuking your soup on the run.

Upon arriving in Newark I move out of turn to first class—to get one last look at the giant. He reaches into an overhead compartment to retrieve his camouflage carry-on case. The guy behind him ducks and I eagerly reach up to assist him so he doesn't knock his squirmy neighbor in the head. I smile up to him—he kinda smiles a friendly giant smirk back.

A Bag of Apples

I grab a chair and scoot up to the kitchen table
where my father-in-law is playing solitaire.
His calloused hands thumb the cards over and
over until the deck is done. This round he wins.
He scoops, shuffles and wraps a rubber band around
the deck of cards and puts them into the breast-pocket
of his overalls. He reaches for two apples from a bowl
on the table. Places one in front of me and the other
he takes a bite of. *You won't believe this,* he says.
I was at the dump and saw this perfectly good bag
of apples just sitting there.
I look at him. He looks at me. When he grins,
I bite into my apple.

The Woman Who Wishes to Remain Anonymous
Bakes a Cherry Pie

My father-in-law and I are eating dinner
with the woman who wishes to remain anonymous.
Swedish meatballs, potatoes, corn and white bread.

You won't believe this, the anonymous woman says.
But I found a container of cherries that I froze in 1978.
They still looked good. So I made a pie out of them.

We've been eating it and haven't got sick yet,
my father-in-law says. *That's the gospel truth.*

There wasn't a lot of freezer burn on them? I ask.

Some, but not that much. She shows me the container
the cherries were in. *And you cannot write about this*
or tell anyone who I am, until you try a piece yourself.

She reaches into the freezer, because she has already
frozen the pie; she doesn't want the leftovers to go to waste.
She thaws two pieces in the microwave.
My father-in-law cuts a piece and eats.

Are you sure it didn't say 1998? I ask.
The woman smiles serenely. I dig in.

What They Do Not Tell Us

...sharing every cold
observing agonies
they cannot tell at home...
　　　　　—Nancy Henry

It bothers me to see my wife get off after her
twelve-hour shift, come home and lie
lifeless on the couch, losing herself in
the television, curling up in a ball.
When I ask her how work was she says,
We got our asses handed to us. People died.

What I'm learning is that there is nothing I
can say or do. I will never know what it's like
to watch a twenty-two-week-old
baby hang on for three more months, then die.
Never know what it's like to scrape dead flesh
from burnt living bodies. Will never know
rising at five a.m. and staying on my feet
until seven p.m. without much break,
without lunch, and, god willing, without error.

Will never know what it feels like to turn code,
stabilize, and then realize I've forgotten
one easy last step. Will never know the satisfaction
of flying to Kentucky or Idaho
from Nebraska in a twin prop
to bring a baby back to life. Will never know
what this is like: *We got our asses*
handed to us. People died.

A Pony for Paige

Paige, you are only four weeks old
and your sister demands she help out.
I hope you know how proud she is wiping
dry skin she calls *crumbs* from your face,
proclaiming to paint another red,
white and black design you can stare at.

Your mother puts the finishing
touches on the barn she has built
in the living room to house the ponies—
blackie Morgan, brown Spirit and white Joe.
I reinforce the support beams, but can't
for the life of me figure out how
to secure the ladder to the loft.

People might think it odd, a barn
in the living room—let them think
whatever they like. Creatures awake
early here. Willow galloping with colts,
fillies and foal across wood floors.

Your eyes open ever so slowly
to peek at this parade of wild animals.
In between rides and morning breakfast,
Willow checks, then checks again, to see
if you are awake. When she finds your eyes
open she cannot contain herself:
Look Daddy, Paige is smiling!

Then back to the mustangs she trots,
taming first one, then another,
waiting as only a child can wait
for the time when they can do the tending,
tugging and pulling together.

The Metal Detector

Through the metal detector and after the pat-down by police, we found our seats on hard pews in the courtroom. There to bail out a "friend" who beat up some innocent bystander, someone who probably looked at him wrong. I felt ashamed when I saw him handcuffed, shirt torn from his Friday night brawl. I was not surprised, though. I was disgusted that I was forking over money for something like this. But, I was in high school, ignorant, and I didn't think for myself. He stood silently as they read what he was accused of. Twice he looked over at us like a pathetic dog. Just as quickly they took him back to jail.

The judge continued to read off names of the accused. We couldn't leave until he was done. A 60-year-old man hobbling on a cane went next. The front of his shirt brown with dried blood—suspect of child molestation. I wanted to throw up. I couldn't leave.

I'm in my daughter's room now. I have learned to think for myself—to do unto others as I'd want done to me. As I tuck her into bed tonight, I wonder: will monsters with canes and bloody shirts interrupt what should be precious thoughts of this world we live in? I cannot follow her everywhere. I can only teach her what to look out for, to repeat over and over never to trust strangers—to think—always to think hard, and for yourself.

MISSING

During the 1980s, twenty-year-old John Joubert was convicted of the murders of two boys in Nebraska. He'd gotten his start in Maine at the age of thirteen when he'd stab other children with pencils, razors, and other implements and found that he enjoyed hurting others. He tried strangling a boy and then when he was 18, he killed an eleven-year-old. Then he fled the town. From a broken home, Joubert had been an angry child, and he discovered both solace and power in striking out at others and getting away with it. In Nebraska, he looked for victims while volunteering in a Boy Scout troop. For him, the torture and murder of young boys was a way to relieve sexual tension. But as with all predators, the experience did not ultimately satisfy, so he would soon plan another.
—Katherine Ramsland, *Crime Library*

John, you have been executed, you
are dead. I am thirty-five years old and
I still can't get you out of my head. I know
why; it's exactly what you wanted.
All the children of Omaha, perhaps
all children, right? There are stories of you
as a Boy Scout leader turned killer,
an Air Force sex ring. A follower.
Perhaps you were kicked like a poor dog
one too many times.

You with your mirrored sunglasses, your
hoodie pulled tight around your head. None of us
will ever forget your police crime sketch
on street poles, milk cartons and store windows.
That Halloween, we went in large groups,
and mothers and fathers stayed close behind,
some even with bats—hoping, praying,
for redemption. It was our neighborhood you
did this in; we wanted it back.

How many nights did I curl up
in a fetal position, staring at my second-story
bedroom window shades?
It didn't matter what our parents said,
we invented worry, never again would talk
to strangers because every one of them was you.

First grade, when I fell on the ice at the bus stop
and an icicle went into my knee,
the bus driver hollering, *Quit your bellyaching.*
Either board or I'm leaving.
He left, and blood oozed as I limped back to
the strip mall in Country Club Village, the apartments
where we lived. A guy came out to help, tried
to reach my folks without luck, and took me
to school where Mr. Shiver yanked my arm
out of the socket for catching a ride from someone
You don't even goddamn know!

That's when I knew my world had changed.
This was the late seventies, peace and love falling
on the cusp of cocaine, and everyone began
living faster and meaner. This was when you John
were living with your nightmares, perhaps calculating
rapes, cuttings and killings.

Ashes, ashes, John—
No
No
No.

Running with Wine

This is what I remember,
and I wish you would go away.
Walking down 60th Street with
Todd, smoking Camels, going
nowhere. I remember you
passing us on the sidewalk,
darting across the street toward
Elmwood Park between dim
street lights, your shadow, running.
Then screech! Brakes. Thud. Bottle
breaking. Exhaust. You lying
motionless on the street. Tires
spinning away. Both of us
standing over you, checking
your pulse, staring at your face—
beautiful, pale. Sirens ringing.
Cops showing up. One of us
pointing out the broken wine
bottle you'd been carrying,
Maybe she's drunk.
The police officer kneeling
down to inspect the bag the
bottle was in. *No. It's corked,*
he said slowly. *I believe
she had plans for this evening.*

South Dakota Bumper Stickers (circa 2010)

Have You Hugged Your Hog Today?

I'M RETIRED

Gone Fishin'

GET OFF YOUR PHONE AND DRIVE

EAT BEEF
The West Wasn't Won On Salad

Horn Not Working
Watch For Finger

Working for an Idiot Free America

You are in INDIAN COUNTRY

REPUBLICAN WOMEN are the life of the party

GUN CONTROL
Means Using Both Hands

This Year I Got a New Gun
For My Wife. Good Trade Don't Ya' Think?

Where the Heck is
WALL DRUG

IF IT FLYS IT DIES

I remember Korea

DON'T LAUGH MISTER. YOUR DAUGHTER COULD BE ON BOARD!

Retired **HOOTERS** GIRL

Ted Nugent

Bow Hunters—**A**gainst—**D**rugs

STURGIS Ride To Live

I LOVE MY WIFE

You Just Got Passed by a Girl (same car) Bite Me
(same car) If You Are Going to Ride My Ass At Least Pull My Hair

Don't Mess with My Country

BAD ASS TOYZ
AREN'T JUST FOR BOYZ

My Drinking Team Has
A Demo Problem

Siouxland Eye Bank
Please Donate

My Other Auto Is a .45

Next time you are perfect try walking on water.

Charlton Heston is MY PRESIDENT

COWBOY UP

You Can Have My Book When You Pry It from My Cold Dead Hands

My Other Car is a BROOM

I'd Rather Be at a Neil Diamond Concert

SUPPORT OUR TROOPS
BRING THEM HOME
HALF MY HEART
IS IN Iraq

Sure You Can Trust the Government
Just Ask an Indian

I know Jack Shit

BOYCOTT Veal

It's Bush's Fault

Fry Cook, Stockade Bar and Grill, Millard, Nebraska, 1985

Fourteen years old on a four-to-nine o'clock work permit making three dollars and fifteen cents an hour scrubbing pots and pans at the Stockade Bar and Grill—*You're not finished yet*—peeling four five-gallon buckets of Idaho potatoes until one o'clock in the morning. Hands scalded a permanent red from stacking hot plates, griddle platters, breaking water glasses—*That's coming out of your paycheck, friend. You know how much each of those glasses costs me? Not another snot-nosed pecker that can't hold on to a sip cup!* Black shoes standing on a black rubber mat, smell of greasy fried chicken and Salisbury steak— brown gravy on a mandatory white-collared dress shirt—*Order up! Order up! Order up! Food's ice cold.* Brown door smacking me in the head, dropping bus carts in the entryway exit. *God damn, boy, you know how to fry a burger? Maybe you won't break so much shit back here. Come over and hold this. When those burgers start bleeding, flip 'em over, and when that side is bleeding smack and squish it down like so. Give me your forearm. Feel this here, here and here—that's rare, medium and done. Now watch that rib eye. He wants it black and blue.*

It's not what you know, it's who you know.

Your voice rattling in my head again,
waking me from my slumber.
These nights I come to in a hot sweat.
This hellish nightmare, back in the warehouse
maintaining the Optical Character Reader
or even worse—sorting endless flats,
smothered by meter machines and INS
green cards wishing I was the guy running
the OCR. You Boss-lady with your thick
eyeliner and glops of makeup, your high heels
two sizes too small, hobbling out
on the floor and barking out orders. These days
Happy Hour can't come fast enough.

My coworker with his hands on Megan's
ass and tits, Sharon in the break room with
a black eye. The floor manager scooting off
for beers for lunch, leaving his dope in the
delivery van. How we survived with our BS
degrees in English and our $6.00 an hour
still haunts me. Our plasma donations and
overnight experimental paid laboratory stays,
writing loaded checks at Fast Bucks until
payday when we'd start the cycle all over again.

I saw you on a billboard Boss-lady
advertising your top-dollar earnings.
It's not what you know, it's who you know.
Isn't that what you always told us?
Isn't that what you're trying to sell us now?

How do you like my M's?

my wife asks. *They are supposed to be birds.*
How about my purple horse? It's bedtime
for Willow, November 1. We are grilling out
and drinking day-old Vampire wine.

Chalk on the bricks. A game of tic-tac-toe—
no winner, no loser. Sunshine, XXOO.
The sidewalk art glows with glee. My daughter's
sandbox toys are strewn across the yard.

It's nine o' clock and, for two more hours,
if Willow doesn't wake, this time is ours.
The cool buzz of the baby monitor,
the cheesy brats bursting on the grill,
the gurgle and kiss.

Would you mind reading this new poem?

How long is it?

I just want your honest feedback.

*Every time I tell you what I think you get
all pissed off.*

You're exaggerating.

*Uh-huh. You really want me to tell you
what I think?*

Please. Usually when you don't like it,
it gets published.

*Isn't that nice. Stir the sauce, it's
starting to burn.*

What?

*In front of you—the sauce. And don't let
the noodles boil too long.*

What about this line...Free those breasts
and their veiny road maps....

*Stop. I hate when you read it to me out
loud. Just give me the damn thing.*

Not if you're going to get all pissy about it.

Fine.

Great. The noodles are all soggy.

I told you.

Yes you did.

Triple Dog Dares

I know a woman who collects stuffed black crows—and I know why.

When I was a teenager, living on Chandler Street, dodging traffic—cess-sliding with my homemade Hosoi-nose Gonzales-back skateboard—my father the actuary stopped me when I finally dragged home, said, *Death comes in threes.* We talked mortality. Risk. Losing a friend. *Threes. That's always been my experience.* I'd like to tell you I slowed down after that talk. It only got worse. I am obsessed with the number **three**. *Threes.* **Three** times I check my wallet because, once, my card was stolen—gone. In front of my very eyes. Right now in my town, **three hearses**—body bags, polished shoes and impending grief. **Three** times I speak to myself until I realize you are staring. Look closer now and I'll try and quit—just *tap tap tap* until the voices, sometimes one sometimes two…I know everything, right now, might be better than fine. It could all go to hell in a basket of **three hand-me-downs**—smash, illness and demise. Can you see the itch? Twitch? **Tic toc… Tic?** Don't look in my medicine cabinet. Don't read the post-it notes behind its mirror. **3:33** I wait by the nearest clock—**wish** and **skin** and **bone**. But also, there are three people I come home to in this house—luv and kin. Three of my favorite words—*sin, win* and *voodoo.* **321 21 1 1 12 123** Why? I have tasted my karma and **triple dog dares**—this I am sure of. I'm still walking from these tricks—unscathed.

Irene Pop. 470 00

When I push through town I notice the double-zeros someone has added to your green census sign—470 **00**. I imagine them—the young couple, just graduated from high school, the Indian summer turning for worse. *Screw it,* he says. Throws the spray paint they used to decorate the sign with in the ditch, grabs her right hand with his left, puts his other on the small of her back—dip—dark, dirty kiss. *Let's blow this one horse.* She smiles, and tells him, *I'll go anywhere you want.* They jump in his rickety '79 Bonneville, hit the corner store for fuel—find some friends on the bridge out a' town who've bought beer. They get out of the car for one last dance. They laugh to themselves and gulp—laugh, gulp, kiss—throw their empties on gravel. *What's your hurry?* one of the local girls says. *You are going to swallow each other's tongues.* That's when they know it's time. They reach for more drinks and head back to his car and jump in. He revs the thing up—stands on the gas.

The Grass Alley

is just beyond my backyard.
I share it with my neighbors.
On morning walks they creep out
between their lilac bushes.
Mrs. McCann, in a light
raincoat and fishnet bonnet,
stops to smell the spring blooms.
As she leans in for a burst of
the flower's spell, she is startled.
A dog growling. A garter snake
warming in the sun. Slowly
she turns and is on her way—
but stops again, moves towards my
overgrown Pocahontas and Beauty
of Moscow, bows her head and inhales.
I hope when I'm Mrs. McCann's age
I'm still stopping to breathe the pleasure
of another new dawn.

Vernon is Taking the Dirty Dog Home

On these common grounds, you hope you never
run into each other again. I daydream
that I'll spot some of you. Holding your child's
hand, running your tattoo parlor, catfishing
in your favorite holler hole—facing your demons
the best you can. I hope I played a part
in some of this, guiding you away from
a place any of us could wind up in
after a few misdirected decisions.

Imagine a greeting from a mother who still
relentlessly milks the Holsteins, imprisoned
on her own farm, the smell of rotten silage,
the burden of not having enough time.
She will be waiting at her threshold,
door wide open for you.

Imagine the toy brontosaurus on laminate flooring,
its head pointing to your child's bedroom.
You will be welcomed again.

When you, Vernon,
board that Greyhound bus to the halfway house,
keep your head high. With smart time, you'll have
only six months to go. I've been instructed never
to get too close to any inmate. But I'm your teacher,
and I'm afraid that's just not possible. Tonight,
like most nights, I carry you home.

"Makes for 4 Persons"

There are secret ingredients in Chinese food;
this is why most Chinese people are slim.
This is my thesis statement and I'm here to argue.
I want the recipe. A garlic and ginger
snapdragon mix. The sweet and sour. Your ancient
secret. I want to eat like a king and be hungry
an hour later. Metabolism of the absurd.

I want the neighbors to know when I'm cooking.
Aroma to run through apartment walls,
like when I was ten, and the neighbor girl, Jessica,
who was "dirty knees—look at these" kissed my mouth
and it was all sugar and spice.

I appreciate your effort, my wife says, *but please,
don't try to make Chinese food ever again.*

Live and learn, I guess.

You always say that, too. Just leave it alone.

* * *

Makes for 4 persons, the back of the sweet and sour soup mix says.
Crack one egg and stir in one direction for one minute. Serve instant. Do I
mix the egg first? I am making a quadruple batch to feed the Sunday
masses and they are all praying that I don't mess it up. I beat and
put in four eggs. I realize then, I've blown the show. Little spit wads
of egg float to the surface. And no matter how long I boil the soup
and add all the necessary ingredients, it is over. Time to sell the wok.
Time to throw out the Rangoon wraps. Understand this: a toddler
can make Crab Rangoon, and white men can't cook Chinese food.

* * *

When I was fifteen my father's Chinese co-worker
(his family owned a restaurant of their own)
came over for dinner. Jer-San even brought his mother.
We sat down for a good old-fashioned meal of pork tenderloin,
mashed potatoes, gravy and, surely, some corn.
Jer-San's mother kept saying yum yum. Would shovel
some more food and not come up for air. Then yum yum,
again. Jer-San laughed. Smiled. My father, the chef,
smiled. Jer-San said, *American families always try
and make us Chinese food. They should not try.*

The Day Before You Broke Your Wrist on the Monkey Bars

You scream at me over the roar of the mower.
You want to ride your bike around the block—
by yourself. Here in this tiny town, our street
turns to gravel four houses away. I look up the road
and back to you, kill the engine, tell you not to
talk to any strangers, and I swallow hard.

I know this is one small step, one I won't soon
forget. You, Willow, pedaling away, leaning
into the sidewalk's awkward tilt, training wheels
aching to be free. I cut five rows of fescue—
back and forth, and pause to see if I can spot you
through houses, rounding the block.

I think two words, bedrock and believe.
I keep mowing. Soon you appear, pushing your bike
through the neighbor's lawn. You want a drink and to
go again, alone. When I finish the yard
and put the mower in the shed, I watch you grab
each rung of the monkey bars.

One, two, three, four, five and a half years old—
back and forth, reaching, grabbing, holding yourself
in mid-air without our help.

Mothers—*A Toast*

Young mothers, it is spring again.
Valentines have been sent.
The front doors are ajar, little
faces press against storm-door glass.
Put away the disinfectant wipes
and come out, come out.
Fill porches with laughter. Bring your
mending hearts and concerns.
Free those breasts for these little creatures
to discover. And let this be a *Thank you*
from all of us who dart off to work,
reluctant to look in our rearview mirrors,
who oftentimes forget to tell you
how much it means.

POEMS BY

JIM REESE

Really Happy! NYQ Books, 2014

Ready—Action!

I'm standing in line at the mega-pharmacy, waiting to buy drugs. I know, I don't like this place, but it's handy and cheap. Standing in this slow line, I can't keep my eyes off the prophylactic section. Two young guys with bottles of 5-Hour Energy shrug shoulders, laugh, turn to look at who might be staring at them, joke louder, turn back to the KY and rows of Trojans and Lifestyles while they fondle the Astroglide. *Don't be such a numb-nut,* one says to the other as they snicker and turn their cart down the aisle.

Soon enough, they're back. Intent this time on grabbing the right product. Then off they go, burying their goods in a large half-empty cart that in a couple of years they will fill with formula, baby wipes, diapers, Aquaphor Healing Ointment, disinfectant wipes, lead paint test kits, hand sanitizers, lots of sugar-free juice, binkies, tearless shampoo, a Pack and Play, a bouncy seat, pregnancy tests, colored condoms, acid reducers, Band-Aids, Ativan, peroxide, and tonic. The cart will overflow. That will only be the beginning.

Today, none of that stuff matters as they race for the only male check-out clerk. God willing, he will let them pass through with hard-earned cash without asking for their IDs, and not asking if they need to speak with the pharmacist about practical application, correct procedures, or any other instruction they've never wanted or been given.

Black Words on White Paper

I am grading freshman essays. Too many papers
about exhaustive road trips without hitchhikers.
Anorexia. The death penalty. Abortions.
One about the Future Farmers of America.
You don't have to grow up in the country
to be a member. I never knew that.

Most memoirs about families are dysfunctional.
They always are. But sometimes it still scares me
what students reveal. Like when Carlos writes,

That night, when my father pointed his hunting rifle
at my head and said he was going to put a bullet
between my eyes, I knew I had to say something.
That's when I used my voice to make a difference.

The phone rings and it's Willow. *Dad,* she says,
her voice shaky and exhilarated.
Can I get my ears pierced?
She could have asked for a pony
and I'd have given it to her.

How exciting it is to hear a child's anticipation.
The delight, instead of darkness.

Sunshine, Handcuffs, Plexiglass, Scars

See these flowers, a student says. *They're closed at night and in the morning they open—stay open most of the day. I don't know what they're called. I had these same flowers by my front steps. The stems feel plastic, almost fake. They break easily. We aren't supposed to touch them here.*

You know, one of the prisons they had me at, I could step into a corner of my cell and get a sliver of sunlight. It would hit me right here. He cranes his neck and closes his eyes. *Right here on my face for about a half an hour. That was the only sunlight I'd see. It's mental deprivation. It works.*

Hell, most guards don't know what you're in for. They don't care. We were loaded on a 747 one winter and we were standing on the tarmac without any jackets—bunch of us. Just a t-shirt and orange pants, no socks, no shoes. They had our legs chained at the ankles so tight I was bleeding all over my feet and they were freezing. Scars are still here. He puts his leg onto a bench and pulls down his sock to show me.

You know, I'm no killer or sicko. My whole stint that got me here lasted only five months. That's how long it took me to hit bottom. Hanging out with some terrible people I thought were my friends, and I backslid down the whole way that fast. Meth will eat you up. Fifteen years I'll be down for an addiction I couldn't shake—could have never imagined.

When my daughter used to come visit me, I'd be behind those glass partitions— she'd tell me, "Daddy, roll down this window". I'd say, I can't, honey. She'd ask, "When are you gonna come home"?

Soon, I'd tell her. Now she wants to know the date. She'll be graduated by then.

Still and Silent as Stone

After dinner-count, I see you on the stairwell gazing
out the large turn-of-the-century windows, each pane
a looking-glass into that world where you once belonged.

I never say hello to you. You don't see me looking
down these stairs at your back, your khaki shirt, your gray-
receding hair. I climb the next flight, look out the window

to see if I can decipher what it is you are fixed on.
Parking lot? Midday traffic? Over the fence are homes.
Families racing about. A kid on a skateboard ollies

over a manhole. Two speed-walkers point and chatter
as they chase the wind. But shit, man, maybe
I have it all wrong. I see the Chevys and Fords, hear

the engines call, the glass-pack's throaty cough. Maybe
we're more alike than I thought, waiting patiently,
considering that getaway car.

Thunder-n-Lightning

It's tourney time, and my daughter Willow has just scored
her second run this season. The next batter makes out number
three
and Team Thunder hits the field as I strap the catcher's gear onto
one of the unlucky players. She's already drenched.
It's ninety degrees, muggy as all get-out—a storm brewing.

My wife is in the stands, making faces at me, which is always
a good sign, and our other daughter, Paige, is chasing ground
squirrels with the other kids too young to play. I'm helping coach
and keep score with two other fathers as the girls open up
their first can of whoop-ass against the opposing team.

We fetchin' or catchin' here, girls?—the eight-year-old
third baseman hollers. 1,2,3 we are back to the top
of our line-up, chatter begins. *Can you turn around
like Michael Jackson? Break down like Britney Spears?
Shake it off like Salt-N-Pepa? No you can't!*

With cheeks full of sunflower seeds, these girls are starting
to gel. How beautiful it is to see them come together
as a team, discovering the beauty of the game before
it's ruined by adults. Tonight after ice cream, I water
the red maple, the first tree we've ever planted. The girls run

and chase fireflies. When they catch one, they can't help but
hold it hostage and pull its wings. *I just can't stand to see it suffer,*
Willow says. She grabs the hose and begins drowning the thing.
Soon enough they are off for a new adventure.
As I watch my new As-Seen-on-TV Pocket Hose

ravel itself into a ball, I catch a glimpse of what's left
of the firefly, its cold light smeared on cement,
and I hear on this particularly quiet night,
       the flurry of small wings
               ascending.

Knipplemeyer and Sons, We Lay the Best in Town

Forgive me my transgressions and all the shit I've shared....
—Brent Best, *Slobberbone*

My best friend's dad, the block layer, said,
Hold this jackhammer up for a minute,
you skinny little pecker, and we'll let you come to the job site.

This was the same father we looked hours for, who would turn to us
as the sun shone into the entrance of the bar wherever we were,
Millard, North Omaha, Bellevue, begging him for money for
smokes
or beer, or worst case scenario, to tell him he had to go home.
You stupid bastards. Get a job! Get your fat ass outta here
and take your hippie friend!

We wanted to be men, and we knew even then that
this wasn't the way to make a home.
Searching tavern parking lots for his beat-up rig,
stealing coins from his ashtray. We were wrong then
to say we never found him, never saw a thing.

All those manual labor jobs, busting ass to make a buck
so we could blow it on booze, breasts and skateboards.
We'd tear up our bodies cess–sliding and launching off
ramps onto concrete, trying to impress girls, winding up
on our scab-crusted knees, praying to land our moves next time.

All that language that molded us, all that language we wouldn't
use around others, all those words we took in and dished back
only to each other. When it was late, when we tried to dream
but couldn't shut out the voices—couldn't turn off the noise
of a garbage disposal grinding credit cards, the *Go back to your room*
and go to bed! The sugar bowl against the wall of the IHOP.

We made amends. We realized our families were just as unstable
as the rest. And you know, we say the wrong things in families
of our own now. We scream too much, love too much,
but don't let go.

The Fruit House

—for Neil Harrison

We don't fill out any job app,
just meet the dayshift boss who,
and I'm not kidding you, is
straight-outta-movie-haggard—
inhaling his cancer stick
and blowing smoke right in
our faces, asking, *You gonna be*
here tomorrow at Seven a.m.?
Stepping all over his cigarette butt
like that will teach it a lesson.
Don't be late, is all we hear
when he turns the corner. We aren't.

Carlos and I get there early and watch
one of the guys swallow his girlfriend's
tongue before he gets outta her car, then
everyone else dragging their dead asses
in for this twelve-hour shift.

Carlos is in the egg room. At break
in the pisser he's hacking out loogies
in the sink, saying he's never seen so many
hard boiled eggs—has to breathe
through his mouth as he cuts each one in half
and hollows out the hard yolk.

Screw this place. I'm gonna quit. Making me sick.
Can't quit. I tell him. *It ain't even lunch yet.*

I head back to the salad room
where I continue to rip the cores
out of heads of lettuce.
Hit it like it's some fool's head,
the supervisor says.
I continue to punch and rip
punch and rip, punch, rip, until the cores form
their own little mountain of green in the far corner.

Room supervisor is chain-smoking
and watering the pile of lettuce with a hose.
Prewashed, he says and smiles, spitting
on the floor. One by one the heads
are thrown into this enormous grinder
while women gather at the other end,
bagging and tying, bagging and tying.

Here comes carrots from some other room,
boss man says, *Chef salad,* spits again.
And alls I know is I'm boxing up these bags
of salad and taping them boxes shut until
I can't get untangled and I'm all a mess
with brown packaging tape and boss man
yells to me, *Get out!*
I do. Walk by the egg room, holler to Carlos,
Screw this place! See him smile and throw
his white gown and hairnet on the floor,
and we're gone.

We know we have a few more years of freedom,
before we can never quit a job again.

Jockeying for a Mate

The cover of the new Jockey catalog captures
a man and woman wearing pajamas in a wheat field.
I can't tell what country they're standing in, much less
what state. The clouds look familiar, but it's barbed wire

and round bales here. To be honest, I can't remember
the last sea of wheat I've stood in.
The guy is squinting like he might be staring down a doe,
and the erect woman, she's not interested in him;

she actually looks like she's got her eye on some other buck.
He's got to be disappointed. I mean, really,
what kind of guy chases a woman all the way out that far
into the middle of a wheat field?

Stare too long at the picture, and you see the guy has on
a pair of jeans, the wheat almost up to his waist.
They're not fooling anyone. The woman is wearing
a long-sleeved onesie, which is odd. At the end of the day

do we care more about the guy's legs or hers?
Think too long and you imagine the guy is on a gluten-free
diet, maybe he's allergic to wheat, would die to be
on the cover.

The next day I get the skinny. I examine the catalog again,
there they are, closer this time, at an old
wooden kitchen table, both in new waffle thermals,
and are spoon-feeding each other Cream of Wheat.

Waitress in the Sky

At the Hilltop Diner I watch a man push in his chair and a waitress come to clean up his mess. The hostess rings up his ticket and asks, *You want to leave a tip, Doll?* The man looks over his shoulder towards the table. The waitress's young daughter has come to help play clean-up. *Here's a buck.*

  Well, thank you kindly, sir.

The aura of waitresses has always intrigued men. The working class, firm asses of the women who take orders and bring us food. Let's not forget the allure of the damsel in distress. Of course we're just customers paying for a service. So the fantasy of the highway diner's spicy mama is just that.

Imagine a world of only waiters, their greetings something like this: *Hey, Sugar. Would you like to try the morning delight?* Hear the shocked response: *Excuse me, young man, but what did you just say?* The waiter, stone-cold and speechless, slowly reaches to fill the coffee cup without getting his hand slapped.

I would like whole wheat, lightly toasted, not burnt. You know the difference? Two eggs, sunny-side up—cooked. Bring me my steak black and blue. And one last thing. I'd like some ice water.
Put two lemons in it, Doll—don't just drop them in. Squeeze them like you mean it. You understand what I'm telling you?

  Yes. I believe I do, the waiter says.

  Well then go on now, Sugar.

Shirley Temple and a 7-10 Split

Shirley Temple is on her stomach, spinning on a stool
at Ten Pin Lanes. Her dad is bellied up to the bar
next to her. He orders a shot of Ten High, Budweiser back.
He drops the shot in the Bud and knocks most of it back in one
long pull, grabs the nearest bar rag to wipe off what's left
on his face, and orders Shirley Temple another soda—
with a cherry, of course.

She's only eight. I know this because her parents drop her off
at the pool; she's there all day—her skin brown and baked—
that annoying kid who's always pestering. I realize
I'm sorry for her and start to draw conclusions.

Thing is, I spent many a night in bowling alleys
begging my dad's friends for quarters—used to wet my fingers
and touch metal screws on two side-by-side pinball machines,
serving as a conductor, a live wire. I stole change men threw
by empty beer pitchers to play Asteroids. I've stuck gum
in the holes of more bowling balls than I can count, remembering
that sweet smell of oil on rag, the hand drying machines,
all the while contemplating Mark Roth's unorthodox attempt
to pick up the 7-10 split.

Who am I kidding? I grew up in alleys. From Des Moines
to Omaha to here in this town with its six lanes,
where the ball, just like everything else, still physically
rolls back to you.

Habit

It's just habit, when I pass the guys in the yard.
How's it going? Since I was a kid, I'd ask,
How's it going? to strangers and friends alike.

Today, as I pass men in their prison-issued khakis
and numbered shirts, one stops and says,
Don't you know you're not supposed to ask us that?

Those few seconds we stand face to face, I try to conjure
up what I should say, before a correctional officer
orders him away.

No, I didn't know. How stupid of me not to think
of something smarter to say. Me, the teacher,
who can leave prison any time I like.

The Pulse of San Quentin

San Quentin News is an inmate run newspaper distributing over 18,000 copies a month to all prisons in California Department of Corrections & Rehabilitation. (sanquentinnews.com)

Do you have a chance of ever getting out of here?

Son, how old are you?

Thirty-five, I reply, looking right back into your eyes.
You shift and lean in closer, answer, *I've been in here
since you were five years old. I'm never getting out.*

Okay, I reply, awkward, cold, uncertain.

What I should have said is *I'm sorry.* I realize now
this is home for you—you who have been fundamental
in resurrecting the *San Quentin News* after sixteen years,
been instrumental in changing attitudes inside and outside
the prison walls, been the writer who has found the pen
a mighty fortress.

Buckfever

Deer Runs Through Restaurant

SILVER SPRINGS, MD (AP) *–Montgomery County police say a deer being chased by two dogs crashed through a front window of a restaurant before it was put down in the bakery section of a grocery store.*

It's what you call Buckfever, Maurice the baker says.
Sheriff standin' with his pecker in his hand, .45
in the other. Didn't know to shoot or go blind.
Donuts flying, éclairs airborne, smashing sourdough.
Ronette, from over in the deli, come 'round the corner
to see what the fuss was 'bout, scolding him right there,
he better put that pistol away. Right now or so help me
Vincent—I mean Sheriff—you will pay.

Children runnin', screamin'—snot pourin' out their noses,
goin' blind from all the fussin' and flying frosting and sprinkles.
Don't think she even seen that deer, just a So help me gawd!
I ain't kiddin', this is my bakery for cries sake!

Ronette, *he says,* I need you to remain calm and not move
a hair. *He drew down on that sonofabitchin' buck—*
dropped it like a sack a' feed.

Full Moon Fever

It's 1989, and Tom Petty has packed the Hilton Coliseum
in Ames, Iowa. We've driven too long to see a man on a stage,

too far away to reach, but that doesn't matter. Mom's back in Omaha.
In the middle of the second song of the set, his new hit *Free Fallin'*—

he stops the song on a dime and addresses all the good people of the world
still filing in from the parking lot. *For all you arriving late, my name's Tom,*

and these are the Heartbreakers. And he hammers that D chord on his
Rickenbacker into a chorus of fire I've never experienced. Two guys in front of us

pass a joint and the temptation doesn't move us, not this night.
At least they offered, you say. We are two men in some nose-bleed section

of a palace of hits in perfect tune with our lives. Tom takes his usual break,
and before the lights come up for Act 2, a trunk opens behind his mike,

a laser beam of light shoots up and transforms the stage into a spectacle
of wonder; Tom walks out, reaches in and pulls out his signature hat.

Too soon the encores end and we mosey out to the parking lot—speechless,
in a mist of smoke and vibes. I will go to that night again and again, a fever

and aching that none of us ever let go. We follow a full-moon on I-80
until we can't drive anymore, and we park in the lot of some 24-hour diner.

I can't remember if we ate. Can't remember what dream I was running down.
I remember asking you to pull over, take a break, telling you I could drive.

There was no need to rush home. Not sure what was happening or what
true love was. But it was a haze I didn't mind being smothered in.

South Dakota Bumper Stickers—Redux

My Other 4x4 Has Legs

I love animals, they are delicious

The HICK LIFE

That's What She Said

I like my women like my deer: HORNY

I'd rather be hang gliding

I'm A Hot Tubber

BE THE FISH

I'd rather be riding her, too

I'd rather be CUMMIN than GOING

Save the Ta Tas

If it has tires or tits, it's trouble

I can muck 30 stalls before breakfast!
What can you do?

Absolute Car Credit

MORE COWBELL

Gayville Fire and Rescue

**If the Fetus You Save is Gay,
Will You Still Fight for Its Rights?**

Will Brake for Explosives!!!

Get the HELL Outta the WAY, Grannie's late for BINGO

Socialism Sucks

Native
Thunder Clan

                                   Lock 'em and Drop 'em
Red Hair, Don't Care

          Water Boarding is for Pussies

Green Bay **Fudge** Packers

          IF YOU DON'T LIKE WHISKEY, HUNTIN' AND
          STRIPPERS, DON'T COME HERE

Keep Honking, I'm Reloading

BEWARE THE MARE!

                                   Save a Cow, Eat a Vegetarian
                                   Eat More Kale

BACK OFF, City Boy

ALARM = Mastiff

          **IF YOU CAN'T STAND BEHIND OUR TROOPS,
          FEEL FREE TO STAND IN FRONT OF THEM**

SAVE the *Boobies*

Cowboys for Christ

I **MISS** President Reagan

My other tractor is my neighbor's

It's not the destination, it's the journey

Silly Boys,
Jeeps are for girls

My kid defends freedom for your honor student

I LOVE CONNIE

My horse bucked off your honor roll student!

Somewhere in Texas, There's a Village Missing an Idiot

Ain't Nothing Meaner than a Marine, 'Cept his Mamma

If You Think My Truck is Smokin',
You Should See My Wife

Fishing stories told here. Some true.

ANGRY. NEED A WEAPON. PRAY ROSARY.

I'm not tailgating, I'm drafting

I Like it Dirty
I Like 'em Dropped
Let's Do It

I was normal...
then I bought my first horse.

Behind every good horse
is a human...cleaning up!

If you're gonna ride my bumper
you'd better put a saddle on it!

96

Will You Sell That Eyesore?

Every summer I lived with my grandparents on Leisure Lake,
outside of Trenton, Missouri, in a house we called a cabin,
built with the help of squirrels like me. Though I was old enough
to know better than to use the leftover gallon-and-a-half

of tan house paint to customize his beat-up Chevy pickup,
my grandfather, who was spray-painting the truck's paneling
with high-gloss brown he had left over from the gutters
insisted that I utilize the same brush I'd used on the garage

to paint the cab, doors, and rust. *This truck has got a lot
of life left in her yet.* When men have their hands on cans
of spray paint they go to a different world, a place where
everyone's an artist. *A little bit more here, and here—*

shine her up like new. For most of an afternoon, we painted,
then watched the truck dry. *Lookee here; pretty as a plate.*
Can't even see the streaks, he said. *Ma will be tickled.*
Matches the house and everything.

Ink

Fifteen out of twenty-two guys in the class are inked. Blue black brands—their inimitable statements. One of my student's forearms is a mess of calligraphy, and when I lean down to read his arm horizontally it says LIFE—when he turns his arm upside down, DEATH. Interesting, I say out loud, and it is. Someone put a lot of thought into that. I ask the other students in class to write down their tattoos on a piece of paper, or show me if they prefer. One asks, *Do you have a tattoo, Dr. Reese?* And I put my leg up on the desk and pull up my pant leg, push down my black sock. GONZO. *What does that say? Gonzo? What's that supposed to mean? It means immersing yourself in the story—instead of writing about someone getting a tattoo, you go get one yourself and tell everyone how it feels to be permanently marked.*

Outside this prison, body art is a statement—a mark of authority. *M.O.B. Money Over Bitches; Loose Lips Sink Ships; What Is, Will Be; Loyalty; Born 2 Fail, Destined 2 Succeed; Death B4 Dishonor; Soldier, Virgin Mary, Jesus Christ, Heart, Rose; Wild Wild 100's; Suckafree.* And on the eyelids of one man there are two tattoos that read—*GAME OVER.*

In here, as I watch men peel off layers of themselves, stripped of freedom, some trying to find redemption, I still question them. *Who the hell has the tattoo—Fuck the ATF DEA US Marshals?* I see X put down his head, his face turns red. He slowly raises his hand, kinda grins. *I seen it,* another classmate of his says. *It's on his back.*

And immediately I flash back to high school, in some cramped apartment drinking a forty with god knows who, some Nazi punk with SKINS tattooed across his forehead backwards. I tell the class the story. How we all hated the kid but didn't know what to do. They laugh. Cuss under their breaths. Shake their heads. X is deadpan, looking out the iron window.

Relaxer

In Chicago O'Hare, I stop at the back-rub place,
pay my twenty dollars for the "Relaxer."
I'm peering over the privacy partition, attempting
to see which woman I would like to rub me down,

trying desperately to avoid the man to my left
cracking his knuckles. *You have back problem?*
No, I tell him. I'm back up on my toes gawking
at the pretty women rubbing their hands through hair—

their soft, delicate touch. *Come. Lajos will fix your back.*
he says. I've already paid the twenty bucks, so I do what
I'm told. *If it hurts too much, tell Lajos. Lajos will fix*
back problem. My face is buried in a paper towel,

my body slumped in a portable massage chair.
He starts in, elbowing me in the back and grinding
on my spine. *You carry stress here*, he says. *And here.*
He starts deep rubbing the sides of my lower back and then

does some number on my arms—trying to shake out
my enormous biceps. *Hey, Lajos,* I say through the paper towel.
That's where I release my stress. He chuckles. *Chicken wing.*
I paid good money for this private intrusion, a foreigner

rubbing, tearing at my limbs. All I hear is the security level
is yellow, elevated, significant risk—remain cautious, and
some funky relaxation music, and Lajos saying, *Here,*
much pain. Lajos fix. To be honest, I don't want him to stop.

He rubs my scalp, stretches my arms in directions they've never
gone before, claps his hands. *Done. Like newborn, yes?*
You bet. I tell him. And I'm off, all bright-eyed,
for new destinations.

Saluting Lieutenant Jones

Make no mistake. We are experts in the application of violence... Your
conscience should be clear. Your honor should be clean.
 —from *Hell and Back Again*, a film by Danfung Dennis

Good morning ladies and gentlemen.
On behalf of Delta flight 3144,
I'd like you to help me welcome
our United States soldiers flying with us today.
In line for our security check,
families surround us in camouflage
and tears. Young children clutching
onto fathers, and mothers,
departing for active duty.

I don't know why we gotta keep sending these kids
over there to the Middle East.
We have to take care of ourselves, this country.
Two guys behind me comment.
Hell, they been fighting wars over there
for thousands a' years.
Ain't anything we can do to change them.

On this forty-four minute flight to Minneapolis,
C-17 Globemaster all enormous and gray,
carrying kids to Afghanistan—to hell—
US Air Force Lieutenant Jones is in tears.
Occasionally I look between seats to see
if he's okay. Now he's red-faced.
Now he's stone-faced. I want to reach back to him,
find out his first name. Buy him a drink.
Get him bombed out of his mind so he can forget
for at least a short amount of time.

Hell, Jones, I'm sorry no one is talking.
These are just black words on white paper.
We're all scared to know what's happening here,
what's maybe ending now.

100

Hard Nutcracker

I slept through "The Nutcracker" in third grade.
Now, nearly 40, I'm dancing in the ballet.
So what color tights do you get to wear? My colleagues ask.
For the past two months I've been catching myself
standing pointe in the kitchen while stirring the goulash.
At any unsuspecting sound, I turn to check the wall behind me.
My students have begun staring strangely at me. One says,
Did you sprain your ankle or something?

All the world's a stage, and all the men and women
merely players, I tell them. *Metaphor. Shakespeare.*
Look him up. And if you must know, I'm dancing in the ballet
with my daughter and wife.
I bow and flutter my wrists to show them I am not embarrassed.
You can dance! Another student exclaims more than asks.

I want to mention the six-degree separation I have
with Kevin Bacon. Remind them of the first *Footloose.*
How I danced in front of the movie screen up and down the aisle
with my mother because we could as the blockbuster ended and
the credits rolled. Show them old Run–D.M.C. videos—
find my boom-box and pop a few locks. But instead I tell them,
There are things you will do for love, someday, young
grasshoppers, that will make all the difference.

During these six-hour dress rehearsals the girls are in the wing
crying. Girls backstage practicing splits, girls in the ring, fighting...
Girls on stage dreaming, girls bending and pivoting,
re-lacing satin pointe shoes to appear weightless and sylphlike.
All the world's a stage, I whisper to my daughter, before it's her cue.
They haven't kicked us out yet.

Where I'm Going, Where I've Been

Some days in the education building
at this prison camp you'll find a man tracing
one of the large maps of the United States
with his finger. Sometimes groups huddle
around the maps, talking about adventure,
reminiscing about childhood birthplaces. One exclaims,
Here's *where I'm gonna go once I'm outta here.*
Find me a job and do it up right.
Gonna be a father this time 'round.
I stand at the map during break.
I trace the Missouri River south. Find its confluence,
the Mississippi. Follow it down and down.
An inmate walks by, says, *Anywhere but here.*
Anywhere but here.

Medley

I work in a prison. My three-and-a-half-year-old daughter, Paige,
knows this. People have told her, *Your daddy works at a prison.*
That's where they put mean bad people. Someday, I will tell her
what it is I do there—that I teach men to write, to help them
come to terms with their emotional instabilities.

Today, when she asks for more chicken nuggets,
I ask her if she has finished her vegetables.
Well, actually no. I am saving them, she says.
I nod. *Actually is such a big word, I'm so proud of you.*
But actually, you'll have to eat some vegetables first,
or you will have to go to prison.

I get up from the table, lower my head and put my hands behind
my back. I pretend to walk in shackles.
They cuff you up, and you'll have to eat your vegetables without
any silverware. I keep pacing around the kitchen and stop to bob
for vegetables from my plate. I come up for air, a mess
of lima beans and peas. Paige begins to cry.
Her sister, Willow, who is seven-and-a-half, says,
That's not funny, Dad.

Not only have I reinforced their fear of prison. I have ruined
vegetable medley. Being a father isn't easy. Being funny isn't either.

New Folsom Prison Blues

There are few words for
Razor on flesh—for Scream.
Black. Blue. Cut. Wet.

I see some of you bandaged
at the wrist, forearm, belly, throat.
You are cutting to get out.

If we treat men like animals
they'll eventually start
to chew their way out.

We know this, now.

Gothic Chic

There's always a sun
in my daughters' drawings.
Big and yellow with sharp rays
extending from its core.
Two or more bizarre people
always holding hands,
and more than likely
an awkward-looking heart
in the picture. An upside-down
triangle split, where two halves
make a whole. Thank God for that.
What if they only painted gray haze
and smoke stacks? Black cats?
What if all they wanted to do
was use their periwinkle
for lipstick, and then devour
the crayon?

Prison Thermos

I'd never given much thought to a thermos.
But here, they are trademarks. Your identity.
Walking with instant freeze-dried coffee, milk
on ice, Tang. Decals stuck to your insulated canisters.
Some with family trees and longing eyes.
A picture of your child in second grade,
bright-eyed, big glasses and missing front teeth.
Others with cut-outs from magazines. An ass. A G-string.
Leather breasts on the back of a Harley. 6x6 antlers.
Trophies toasting these ounces of freedom
they haven't yet stripped away.

Wishing Well

Each one of us makes a myth of the soul we imagine ours.
So mythic we'll never vanish.
　　　　　　　—Kevin Clark

In the hallway I find a note on the floor:
I hope my mom and DaD don't Diy forevre.
My daughter does this sometimes, leaves notes.

She tries to ignore me as I hold the letter
in my hand and ask, *What's this?* She turns her back
and acts disgusted. I don't push the issue.

All day I approach the note again from different
angles. Is she scared? Has she been watching too much
TV? How do I tell a six-year-old that we all die someday?

Later, after exhausting myself with the right
thing to say, I think soon enough she'll want me dead—
not seriously gone for good, just out of the picture.

When she's a teenager, all that freedom she'll be aching for,
like the other day, screaming at me, *Dad! I can get out of the car
by myself! Thanks for the ride.* And she's out of the car, running

down the small hill and into school, her enormous pink backpack
smacking the backs of her calves. A friend of mine once said,
You can't be friends with your kids.

I know what he means; we can't just be friends.
That'll come down the road, when they're gone to train orcas
and wrestle with the other predators of the sea.

I also know I'll never stop being their father.
As I get older, I'll still need them to ask me for advice.
Like, *What the hell is a basin wrench for?* Or,

Why do you care about that so much? I realize our
relationship will continue to evolve, like mine with my
father and mother, how we occasionally still butt heads.

I never understood their parenting back then.
Now it seems a bit more clear.

Down

i've been down.

Been down since '91.

i've been down goin' on nine years now.

Been down at three prisons. This here's the cream of the crop.

i count my time in Ajax bottles.

You know how many cinder blocks are in my room? 236.

Hell, this is a caste system they trying to run in this country.

Down
Down
Fear Down
Dread walking this flat yard forever.

Ask me how many of us are nonviolent offenders; just ask me.

You know how much money i cost taxpayers since i been down?

i don't know if i can survive. If i leave here, what will i do? What can i legitimately d
to make some money—all these bills waiting for me when i get out. Ain't nothing left
for me out there. Lost it all.

Hell, i'm just a short timer.

That's how i caught my case. Lying to myself every day. Gets easy. Day in day out.
* It's just a lie.*

Man, you don't understand what it's like to be down. You weren't born a crimina.
Man, what you talking about? You weren't born a criminal, neither.

The Actuary

It was the ritual that caught my attention first.
My father's ties neatly aligned. The suits color-coordinated,
pressed and hanging in his closet. Before morning rush hour,

this man appeared in the kitchen spinning the gold
combination code of his briefcase—that familiar pop
of air and business inside. Then the double-checking of its

contents, the vacuum-sealed closure of an actuary.
Every time I asked what he did, he'd roll his eyes
and look at me deadpan. *It's complicated. You wouldn't understand.*

You see, he never brought work home with him. It stayed bottled
inside that briefcase. My mother on the other hand,
who always worked late, uncorked her day's dilemmas

at dinner with a red zin or noir. I'd remember
her co-workers' names, often pretending that my goulash
was the insides of their brains. *Look mom, I'm eating*

that dick Jerry's brain. How cool and collected one side
of the table seemed, while those of us on the other side
were dripping daggers and gulping blood.

On the days I pressed my father, he'd say things like *risk.*
That he analyzed future financial events.
Predictions. Mortality. Insurance. Loss.

Part fortune-teller. Part advisor. But all math.
You never heard my father say actuaries were super-heroes.
The headhunters who called for him on a regular basis,

when he refused to answer the phone anymore,
asked me time and time again to leave those messages
for him. Work is the ritual that drives my family still.

Even me, the college professor with my sports jacket, tie
and razor-burned neck. My daughters now leave me Post-it
notes in the closet: *Dad, wear this ty today. I hope it matchs.*

I'm a teacher. I advise. I predict. I analyze and hypothesize.
There's a crystal ball on my desk. Oh, baloney.
On my desk is a flying pig. I can't predict anyone's outcome,

but I'm learning to believe in all this paraphernalia.
When I stare at that boar long enough,
I'm reminded how far anyone can come.

The Blues in Jeans

When I found the sewing needle
in the crotch of my newly hemmed jeans,
I was troubled. Not for the business
that had gone unharmed, but for my
overall well-being.

My mother-in-law had done the sewing.
Perhaps forgetful, perhaps not.
An instinctive shriveling rendered
my jeans somewhat roomier
than I remembered.

General Equivalency Diploma

Hey, I passed—I really did it!
Two inmate students high-five each other.
Way to go man! I told you you'd do it.
The one pats the other on the back.

White men Red men Yellow men Black men
all happy to be graduating. Their smiles
frozen on Polaroid—ear to ear to sky,
soaring alone now—*FREE.*

GED test result day is always fun here,
the Education Director says.

Really Happy!

And, like me, he misses the old days, when talking to yourself meant you were crazy, back when being crazy was a big deal, not just an acronym or something you could take a pill for. I liked it when people who were talking to themselves might actually have been talking to God or an angel. You respected people like that.
—George Bilgere

Take highway 81 north, just over the Missouri River bridge, and merge onto Broadway—this is river city—dirt's grime and chime. There he is with the worn jacket, sun-faded red, white and blue hoodie.

Listen. He's belting his guts out again, all the way up these four lanes. Broadway is humming with cattle trucks on their way to the world's largest livestock auction, jake brakes and texters—all of these pilgrims haulin' ass north to a colder Dakota or scoopin' the loop out of boredom. You can hear him above the din. Some days he's pedaling and now he's be-boppin' on foot, singing what sounds to be Dylan's *Tambourine Man* or is that Sly's *THANK YOU FALETTINME BE MICE ELF AGIN.*

The other day my daughter asks, *Is he wacko?* I tell her, *He's having a good time.* Today, because of our own cabin fever, we are packed in the car looking for him—windows down, a cold January wind filling the cab. There he is turning onto 25th, then Fox Run Parkway on his way to the global super-center for a new pair of socks; or maybe to some human behavior center where they'll ask him to take off his headphones and talk with the others. We cheer him on; let him take his time at the crosswalk, his right hand waving and left hand clutching the radio. He doesn't miss a beat, banging that imaginary snare and floor tom.

That's the guy who saved rock and roll, my daughter says. *Yes, indeed,* I respond. I feel happier than I have in days—my daughters in the back, all smiles, bobbing their heads up and down to their own music. He keeps right on going past the South Dakota tradition, a 12,000 square-foot machine shed where this weekend it's all you can handle crab legs and mountain oysters. He's not after food. He's not stopping at any gas station casino for his cash crop. Doesn't stop at the floral shop—nor does he need a tune-up. He pays no attention to the three whiz kids on the other side of the road playing swords—pissing into the wind. Doesn't seem to give a rip about much of anything except the rhythm of the guitar, that thump thump thumping of the bass, and his own irreducible voice.

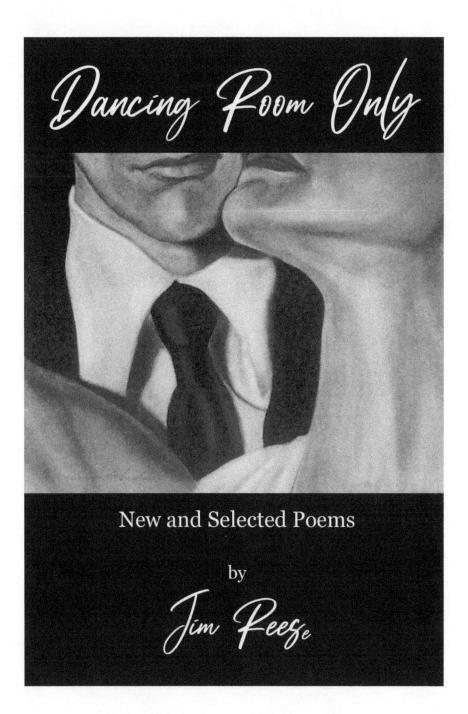

Dancing Room Only (NYQ Books, 2023)

Dancing Room Only

One of those first Friday nights, staring at my inadequate paycheck, I couldn't stop shaking. The bills were due and I wasn't holding enough in my hands. This was twenty years ago, 11th and E Street, where we moved from college to careers—small town to city. I can still see the dim lights of that shoebox of an apartment. One old Murphy bed closet that held everything we owned, where we hid our useless college degrees—and hung your brand-new wedding dress. Our used college textbooks and dual copies of *Beloved* and *Crime and Punishment*. Our wool socks snagging on the splintered wooden floor. The un-insulated plaster walls ached with the wind—water pipes popped and gurgled in the cold. Such character, I thought, with its sconce wall lights and barefoot-claw tub. Sirens and another aimless wanderer outside on the street, sounds that never turned off.

Did we really hate the woman upstairs who partied late nights after her bar shift? I questioned my own bohemian lifestyle, the one I had read so much about—where pain and suffering were part of the process. Me, a wannabe-writer who hadn't done much yet, pleading with the day-shift manager for $7.50 an hour. I'd made more money in high school, telemarketing Omaha Steaks, than I did with a college degree.

We sat at our first computer in a porch room that wasn't heated, typing resumes, trying to type poetry, our story, and their story—our graduate school applications. Always that throb of my heart in my eye-lids that I just wanted to turn off, voices rattling in my head, waking me most nights in a hot sweat. The hellish nightmare that was my life, working in a warehouse, maintaining an Optical Character Reader, sorting endless flats, smothered in meter machines.

Some nights I still see myself sitting on that floral yellow-and-green hand-me-down couch, my body sunk in defeat, the couch engulfing me, my head in my hands. I see you standing there radiant, confident that we would get by. Maybe that was the night I started to believe that even with all my dreams and disillusionment it would work. You

117

and I. The faith you had in me picked me up like it's done so many times since. I can't remember the words you spoke as you turned us to the door, took that antique doorknob and opened it.

Later, we walked downtown, into the Zoo Bar nightlife, and danced our blues and my shame away. How little we seemed to have back then. How much love we've surrounded ourselves with now. How we continue to push through the crowd.

Honey Do List

Shirtless, the men in the neighborhood
put down the remotes, sit upright
in their recliners and come out of
hibernation. It's time to wage war
against noxious weeds in the yard, drag dead
branches and trash cans full of god-
knows-what to the curb, think about
initiating workout routines,
stroll around the perimeters of
the house inventorying
all their stuff and remembering
those honey-do lists—take the holiday
lights down, recycle the beer cans,
replant the garden, repair the leaky
faucet, replace the window, do something
with their no-shave November beards
which are old and itchy. They are
acutely aware of the smell
of grill smoke and Roundup weed killer
in the air, the feeling of fertilizer
pellets in the soles of their shoes.
The neighborhood is green again.
The men buy new razors and take
hedge clippers and chainsaws from
the top shelves of their garages.
Running out of things to cut down
is a pressing dilemma for
the American male. They stretch
out their favorite t-shirts, pulling
them down over their stomachs as they
bend for a few air squats. They floss teeth,
brush grill grates. Windows open,
Harleys humming, it's spring in
suburbia. Women run out
in sunglasses and Spandex, showing
off the first skin of spring, the men
pacing and ready to clear paths,
sucking in their guts, taking deep breaths,
already lying to themselves.

This isn't Dress Rehearsal

It's fifty-three degrees this afternoon. Tomorrow time
will spring ahead. In five minutes the still obnoxiously loud
grade-school bell will alarm the neighborhood.

In line at the chain-link fence with some other fathers who
have shown up, I'm waiting for you, my daughters.
Today, recess should never end.

In two months one of you will leave this place for middle school,
the other will ascend to second grade. Some things never change.
I claw my fingers into the chain-link

that seems so much shorter now. I see the tire-swing, basketball
hoop without a net, blacktop and worn tetherball.
I'm not old enough to wish I were back in your shoes,

not with the math homework you're assigned. But, there's the aching
for some of that freedom. Maybe that's why none of the fathers
standing here say a word.

When I shared the rough draft of this poem in class, a prisoner said,
That's one fence I never minded being behind.
Girls, do you know how much I'm going to miss

these days? This magical moment on all our faces when we see
each other between these boundaries,
waiting to go home?

What a Criminal Teaches Me

One day in my prison class a student told me a story about one of his greatest regrets. What I began to discover was that addiction, in all of its gross and destructive ways, will make people go to extreme measures to fulfill highs of any kind. The student, an inmate in his late twenties, was built, as we say here on the plains, like a brick shithouse. He and I talked briefly at the back of the class. *My grandfather had a Farmall 300. You had a need for hoses for your tractor so you could raise the lift cylinders and tilt bucket with the hydraulics. When the hose was missing—I'm sure he was shocked. When he asked me if I'd seen it, I lied. He said, I've had that tractor, I don't know how long. No one's ever taken a hose off it. What he didn't know was that I used the hose to cook meth. I can't keep feeling guilty about my past. I'm done paying that bill. But I tell you, I wish I'd never took that hose.*

Celebrity

"The whole answer is there on canvas."
—Edward Hopper

Somewhere unnameable,
the gas station neon and florescence
saturate concrete
like a melancholy painting.
A bell rattles as I open the door
into three small aisles, local commodities,
beef jerky, sugar, beer. On the wall
a poster, an enormous photo,
Friday night lights, some high school player
caught mid-air, arm outstretched
in a one-handed catch, a play
the townsfolk still admire
in the God Bless America heartland,
where high school rivalry, Podunk popularity
and a first kiss hang on at great height.
I ask the twenty-something cashier
whose nametag reads Cheyanne,
Is that some local kid?
It is. That's a few years old.
He plays for the Hawkeyes, now.
She seems content.
Cool picture, I say.
Good catch, she says.

Kiss Me, South Dakota

After praying in a football arena with thousands of Lutheran church-camp
teenagers, a cheerful blonde French-kissed me.
Her mouth was bigger than mine.

She told me she was from South Dakota. I didn't know much and thought
I'd just kissed a foreigner. I lived in Omaha, at least three hours away.

I heard South Dakota was bitter and cold.
I must have looked stunned afterwards, eyes closed, mouth still wide open,
while imaginary snapshots in my head

kept looping over-exposed images of a wheat-field—all things golden.
There was a horse. A family in the foreground was staring at me.

They looked hardy—strangely familiar—as if they'd been calling me
there all along. The future, it looked like,
went on for miles.

Surely it was then that I asked if she had her driver's license yet.
I knew I'd need to get back soon and see those people again.

Even If

Checking my rearview mirror for *What ifs*, I let the world and problems that haven't happened yet swallow me. I'm passing people in cars and trucks looking down—not ahead—at the road—convinced that all of us are distracted somehow. Good teachers tell me to enjoy the present, what's right in front of me. *Look forward,* I can hear them say. *Never look back.*

At the prison, I get buzzed in at control and the heavy green military-grade gates slide open. I walk the yard with a correctional officer, and pass through other giant barricades as hundreds of men in khakis, grey sweatshirts, and white t-shirts, scatter on their way to jobs on the compound or to GED classes, to my *Writing for Reentry* class or to the pill line, to prayer groups or to their bunks. I nod and say hello to as many men as I can. I hope my face says, *Smile.* I say, *Onward.* I say, *We are living.* I think, *Breathe.* I hear that little voice say, *You already have the answer. Yearn.*

I'm in a real prison, with razor wire on walls already too tall to climb. No time to stop—no time to look back. One of the only places each week where I live in the present, always alert to my surroundings. I am alive and believe in these men. *Instead of What ifs,* a student in class says, *I'm assuming Even ifs. Then I can keep moving forward.*

What's a Guy Have to do to Earn a Re-Read?

—inspired by At the Dorm by Mandy Kahn

My wife re-reads grocery lists,
our daughters' progress reports,
medical test results, but rarely
wants to read a poem more than once.
This morning she points to a poem
in the newspaper, laughs and says,
This is good. Twice.
I read it then and realize
it's the kind of work people can really read
and carry into their comfortable silences.

The poem is about a country girl
who is obviously falling
for the strong, unkempt, determined
college-boy bumpkin with his arms
full of notebooks and flies buzzing about
his head. Proof that I wasted a lot of years
presuming what a woman wants.

But perhaps a bit of that unkempt boy
carrying all the great ideas
of the world and starry-eyed song lyrics
resembles just a bit of me,
that strange, long-haired city-boy
she married twenty years ago.

I haven't learned much more since then,
my notebooks still scribbled with stained pages.
I know that the trash is mine to take out,
that the heavy lifting and schlepping of large objects
is my job. I've learned to listen with
my two good ears, not the one in between.

Maybe city boys never fully understand
the significance of flies, that a JD 3020 is
a tractor and not a new brand of fortified wine.
Maybe we can't distinguish a Hereford from an Angus,
but we know when to take our shirts off
and how to take our time.

Four Exclamation Points

The first time I had my hands on a steering wheel
was after baseball practice, little league, third grade,
when the whole team would pile into coach Shankie's station wagon.
I can still see the rusty green with fake wood siding on that old beater.
He'd let one of us kids sit on the hump up front
controlling the gas pedal while he kept his right foot on the brake,
both our hands white-knuckling one side of the wheel,
giving us imaginary rein. He'd make sure we were ready, and then
someone would yell, *Give her hell! As fast as you can take her!*

We'd barrel up the neighborhood streets, almost sailing,
skimming the concrete. The kid on the hump reaching
and pressing harder and harder on the gas pedal,
I got the brake kid, don't worry!
The windshield a moving picture show, all blue sky
horizon and the bright, almost hypnotic green
tops of trees and hills, we seemed at that moment to
be climbing—peering in a rearview mirror for
the first time, an array of baseball hats all cockeyed,
a line of eyes showing all their white—open mouths
whoo-hooing our way to the nearest convenience store
where Shankie set us loose in the candy aisle to grab
whatever we wanted, Slim Jims, candy cigarettes, Big Gulps.

One time Charlie Ferguson had the gonads to
take a full-size bag of Doritos to the counter,
and Shankie paid. The unlucky cashier rang the team
up and we climbed back in that beast and were off again—
some new knot-head almost driving, with Shankie's big
hairy left hand at ten o'clock and a couple
of much smaller hands at two. Everything we were doing
was wrong and *Totally right on man!* We had wheels to prove it.

Yoga on Death Row

Training at San Quentin prison I had access almost everywhere. Inside 4 ½ ft. wide, 7 ft. high, and 11 ft. long cells—the size of your typical walk-in closet. In the huge kitchen where a man stands on a ladder stirring a cauldron full of spaghetti sauce with an oar. I was escorted to medieval rooms, a 164-year-old cavern in the exercise-yard. Even condemned row, where a longtime guard said, *The men sentenced to die aren't animals. They've made some horrible decisions. Some premeditated.* At a cocktail party that evening, I met a person who taught yoga to men on Death Row. *They are human beings,* he said. It was odd to hear this with a glass of red wine in my hand. It was different from the fear I still feel, the anguish I still possess over my high school friend who was raped and killed, the tight knot in my heart that every parent has, the horrendous feeling of knowing if that happened to my child what I might do. An eye for an eye while the Pinot Noir stained my tongue. Uncertainty when the glass was empty.

At the Eight-Hour Work Meeting with Bathroom Breaks and a Light Lunch Provided

You watch a glass of water in front of you perspire. A tapping foot under the table—another nervous twitch. The blonde in the tight skirt next to you scribbles *Born To Be Wild* on a yellow legal pad and yawns. *Well, we all know what the real elephant in the room is*, trumpets the man in charge. *Let's not be off a hitch here.* He waves his right arm flush with the vast horizon outside the huge picture window, which seems so distant now. *Let's calibrate.* His good 'ol boy vernacular continues, all the while grinning like a mule eatin' briars. It's clear to you that the pachyderm in the room is standing on his last leg— reaching. *I'm astonished at the elements of power this position entails.*

They're just window dressing, a VP says, sitting up straighter, reassured and red-faced in the posh chair. The designer leather elbow pads of his sports jacket act as suction cups as he tries to raise his arms to emphasize his point. Under her breath the blonde says, *At least they know how to dress!* She checks her text messages and drops her vibrating iPhone into her lap. There's a charge in the room. Or was that an ass suffocating a seat? The fake plastic plant in the corner of the room looks dead.

You look out the window. You remember stopping once in Erwin, Tennessee where legend has it they hung the circus elephant 'Big Mary' with a crane large enough to lift locomotive boilers. She had stomped her trainer. Erwin, now known as the town that hung the elephant. You Google Big Mary, because you are thinking of showing the picture of the elephant to the woman next to you. The roadsideamerica.com article reads: *Over 5,000 spectators showed up to watch the elephant hanging. Big Mary was positioned beneath the crane and then yanked aloft by a chain around her neck – which promptly broke and sent her plummeting to the concrete, knocking her unconscious. A daring spectator, not wanting to disappoint the crowd, dashed forward and reattached the chain. Big Mary was hoisted again, and this time justice was done.* You remember the Hanging Elephant Antique Gallery once sold Big Mary t-shirts. You're pretty sure, although the town has established a nearby elephant sanctuary, you will never go back there.

We need a little steak with all this sizzle! A razor-burned neck says, snapping and cracking as if to re-emphasize a toughness rooted deep within the spine. Without fuss, a small astute man stands. *We've sent out the samples and have to wait until we get the results of the feelers.* *The feelers,* someone mumbles. A few people nod their heads. You reach for your full glass of water, tiny ice crystals slowly dissecting themselves from the last large transparent cube which has risen to the top and slowly grown thin, all of the particles falling away gracefully, free and forever into a clear unknown.

A Ballerina and Her Father in Line at the Coffee Shop

Twelve years old, she begins spinning.
I admire her audacity
to dance anywhere she likes,
tuning out distractions,
like the man behind us
articulating abbreviations into his iPhone.

Young lady,
we can't have any dancing in line.
It could disturb the others.
Says Darla, the barista, who seems
distracted by her own tired fingers
spinning the wand, pulling the shot,
drizzling the caramel into her signature
tulip, clearly not experiencing
the exuberance of youth
we all possess.

Some days I'm Darla, but more often
I'm awestruck at the beauty
of life's little moments,
and I spin sometimes, too.

Machine of Interest

I'm at a stoplight in my town waiting
with the traffic in front of me, everyone taking
their sweet time staring into their laps, checking
their texts, posts, playing, swiping, left or right.

I'm singing to the windshield as fall foliage
on the sugar maples burst yellow and orange,
the leaves letting go and falling to the ground
where they lean on their elbows in dark

perfectly manicured grass, gazing into the horizon.
They no longer cling to branches and are ready
to be blown by any machine of interest.
The stale-coffee-worm-dirt aroma of fall

fills the air. The humidity-cloaked windshields
begin to fog. A single leaf yearns, another thin-skin
shivers. This is the kind of day you ask complete
strangers, or say to yourself, *You getting all this?*
The light has turned from red to green, the traffic in front
wakes—
                    rhapsody.

Real Mayonnaise

This morning, early, their youngest daughter, my wife, rushes from room to room, plugging in the iron, checking the time. Staying home, I'll get the girls to school and back; I can't miss work. That's my excuse. My father-in-law will wear his black work shoes to the funeral, the ones with the thick soles, the only ones he still feels comfortable walking in. He'll grab his nicer cane that he keeps next to his bed. My mother-in-law will hem and haw over a blouse and the right color slacks for the three-hour drive to the big city, their daughter at the wheel of their car. That my mother-in-law will bring along a road map and a plastic hand-held compass comes as no surprise.

When my wife returns from the trip she knows about everyone in town who now has a condition. Says she received a detailed report about every noise in their car and where it's coming from. Tells me how her dad interrupted and gave the play-by-play of farmers in the field planting too deep. *When we stopped for gas on the way home Dad said, "Just give me ten minutes to get outta the car."* She smiles at me and hands me a bag of sliced ham on cocktail buns spread with butter and real mayonnaise that her mom packed for the journey and no one ate.

At the City Pool, Age 45

I take off my shirt and spray Coppertone Sport onto my unevenly hairy chest, confident because I've spent a lot of time lately in the gym exerting myself. My ten-year-old daughter says, *Dad put your shirt back on; that's weird.* Shortly after, her vibrant mother smiles and unveils a pulsating body of prowess, muscle, tone. A man shaped like a potato sitting under a nearby canopy with his paperback in his lap pulls down his sunglasses to get a better look. I'd be lying if I said these glances didn't bother me. The bubbly, yet slightly annoyed college lifeguard in her too-tight emergency-red bathing suit turns and looks in my direction. At least that's what I tell myself. My wife smiles serenely and gently brushes my shoulder with her skin. The lifeguard begins spinning the long lanyard her whistle is attached to a little faster.

I'm at this pivotal point in my manhood, middle-aged according to Wikipedia. Old enough to give up, young enough to change. I know I'm not invincible; gravity will eventually make sure of that. Regular visits to the gym for sanity, sweat, and an honest-to-god grunt will help.

What would life be without desire? Without vitality? We are all animals. Mating is the first call. Always the attraction. Lust, like work, like love, is a four letter word.

It's Just a Job

I'm talking to a crime reporter about my work in prisons, I tell him most of the time I feel like I'm fighting an uphill battle. About three fourths of the staff don't like to see me enter the facility because I'm an English professor and I teach inmates how to come to terms with their emotional instabilities through writing. I tell him I teach at two prisons within a 50-mile-radius of my house that were colleges forty years ago.

Most prisons are in small communities, and people see them as an employer. They don't care about rehabilitation, he says. It's a job. That's it. They understand crime from what they see on TV and read in the paper.

I flashback to a job application I had to fill out at the state prison. There was a question at the end, and you had minimal space to write your answer. The question: What do you see your role as here at the prison? I wonder how many applicants truly wrote: to help rehabilitate.

What the Guy Dressed as the Statue of Liberty Outside Fast Taxes is Really Thinking

All bombs bursting.
No ramparts or rocket's red glare here, people.

***

Here I am with my billowing robe—disguising what's underneath.
Some days I can't tell if I'm headed to a toga party or here to save
the world—standing with my broken shackle and chains,
my right foot raised to start walking again.
What's a person to do with a limp crown and bogus torch?

***

Could be worse. At least I'm not an Oscar Meyer wiener again.
No one ever takes a hotdog seriously.

***

Yeah, up yours, too. At least I have a job!

***

And here comes STRANDED.
IN NEED OF HELP.
TRYING TO GET HOME.
She told me last week, *At least I'm not the one collecting taxes.*

***

Mobile telephone booths. *Stop texting and drive, people!*
You aren't that important. I mean, look at me.
I've been from sea to shining sea!

***

8 one-thousand, 9 one-thousand
10 one-thousand,
turn.

***

Slug Bug Green!

***

Suffering from friction-related skin irritation?
New Gold Bond Friction Defense reduces chafing
to soothe and comfort your skin. Gold Bond Powder feels
like a thousand angels blowing on your balls.

***

All you can eat liver and onions. That ought to bring them running.

***

Another marquee for a gun show. Every time I turn around,
it's a gun show.

Advice

Rest, the nun says,
*is a dirty word
in your house.
You need some.*

2nd Grade Parent Teacher Conferences

My daughter's 2nd grade teacher says, *I thought this week she'd definitely get something wrong. We were working with contractions on the quiz. It took her a little longer but she didn't miss one. Same with her math.* I can feel my mouth open and my wife knee me under the tiny table we were encouraged to sit at. *We were studying model regrouping for addition-how many tens and ones in a sum. She finished her work perfectly in no time.* In my mind, my ass falls off the miniature plastic chair, and I lie there looking up at the mobiles of our solar system. The eight planets—didn't there used to be nine? The moon. *Thank you,* I say, to the shooting star trailing in the corner of my eye.

My Mother-in-Law and the Manhunt

NIOBRARA, Neb. –A police officer has been assaulted at the low-income housing units while attempting to arrest a suspect on a warrant. The suspect was able to disarm the police officer and point handgun at the officer before leaving with the gun on foot into the river bottom area along the branch of the Niobrara and Missouri river.

I'm driving my mother-in-law
to the eye doctor for laser treatment.
We talk about preceding presidential elections.
Gun control. Bi-partisanship. I make no jokes.
She gives me no stares.

She says, *I read in the paper that fella they're after
is 5-10, 150 pounds. He's not that big of a guy.*
She's a farmer's widow now, born in the Dirty Thirties,
when desperate people must have seemed
almost common.

*I had a dream about him last night. That he showed up
at our place.* We look out at the dirt road before us,
ruts veering towards the ditch as we reach the crest of a hill.
*I told him, you can come in and sit down. If you
put that gun away, I'll fix you something to eat.*

Public Paranoia

In waiting rooms across America, used magazines with people's addresses on the covers are blacked out with permanent marker by generous and paranoid people who are fearful that someone will find out they subscribe to *Popular Mechanic* or *Cosmopolitan*. Afraid that someone will read their address, drive to their home and say, *I found your magazine in the waiting room. I can't believe you of all people had this article*—5 Guaranteed Ways to Enjoy Your Ride—*dog-eared*. Today I bring a month-old magazine to my creative writing class at the prison. I show it to the SOE, who approves it and fills out the necessary paperwork. I take the magazine to the prison library, get it stamped EDUCATION, but forget one last step. So it's no surprise when a student says to me, *You might want to black your address out. Most of us are good people here, but you just never know.*

Square Bales

Almost seven and eleven, I still try to cradle you both,
carry you off to bed when you fall asleep in front of the TV,
or in the car after another long road trip to see family.
The only problem is you're each too long to fit through your bedroom
threshold, a limp arm banging against a door frame, a flaying foot.
Each of you heavier than a square bale. Most people are. You're dead
weight, your bodies relaxing as I gently drop you into bed.
Before I do, I still try to curl you up to my chest, like when
you were five and nine, one and five. All this weight reminds me
of the picture of the complete stranger I took and hung on our fridge.
A large man cradling the biggest produce in Lancaster County,
wearing his *#1 Grandpa* mesh feed cap, and a watermelon smile.

Death Penalty

During the eulogy for a nun,
the priest relates, *In the ambulance*
on her way to the hospital
sister stated that she would give
her pain for a successful end
to the death penalty in South Dakota.
A nun sitting in the hard pew
next to me, Kleenex tightly
balled in her left fist, blue-green
veins swelling in her luminous skin,
whispers, *That's so like her.*

　　　　　　　　—for Sister Eileen O'Connor

Right on Time

I'mrunningmythreemilesaroundtheindoortrack,likeIdomostnights. Routine, mundane, and all nine-minute mile splits. I can't seem to go faster. Thin, too pale, men arrive in swim trunks pulled high on their bellies. They cannonball into the pool—acting like kids fresh off the bus on summer break. Their supervisor waves to the lifeguard on duty who absently spins the cord of his whistle around his index finger. Some of the men grab bright-colored rubber basketballs and shoot hoops. Some beam with laughter, spitting mouths full of water, becoming underwater mermen.

One twenty-something guy always slips into the shallow end and squats, his chest and thighs pressed tightly together. Left hand acting as a ladle, he scoops a handful of water, raises it over his head, and fingers dangling, pours a slow spigot of the chlorinated water down into his cupped right hand.

Tonight, he cocks his head to the left, where the swim team practices the backstroke, balancing plastic pop bottles on their foreheads. Exercises in grace that look so easy from a distance but surely take precision and patience. *See,* he seems to say. *Do you see that? How beautiful we are.*

I stop to catch my breath. I'm 46 years old. Maybe no longer as graceful as I picture myself. My body soaked with sweat. There's some grey in my hair. My daughters are on the verge of braces and breaking rules. Everything, I guess, is set to go.

Fore!

An estimated 4.5 million adults are under community supervision,
nearly twice the number of people who are incarcerated in jails
and prisons combined. Prisonpolicy.org

This morning I pull open the dark curtains in my bedroom.
It's sunny and the golf course right beyond my backyard pops green.
The prisoner with khaki pants, here-I-am-orange t-shirt
and INMATE big, bold and unflinching on his back
is mowing the grounds.
The INMATE, in his public pillory uniform looks with disdain
as a golfer tees off and yells just loud enough that we hear the faint,
Fore!

Freedom. Commotion. A beautiful mirage. Birdie or bogey.
The fairways perfectly mowed. Men astonishing themselves
with mulligans.

Going Up?

Monday morning I succumb to the elevator and the non-trad with her luggage of books on wheels. *So what do you teach?* she asks, trying to make polite conversation. *Writing. Creative writing*, I add, because I always feel awkward saying I'm an English professor, a title which still intimidates me. *I'm not a big fan of books*, she says, white-knuckling the handle of her luggage. *Daddy always said, there's no money in poetry.* The elevator slowly grinds to the second floor. The third. I study our warped reflection in the stainless-steel door we're facing, which is now a funhouse mirror next to a wall of numbers, an alarm, all in braille for the visually impaired. Amusing thing, besides being in this elevator with this mature student, I'm used to this exchange. To her, I'm like actuaries and morticians,—ex-cons and cops, unknowns in her world. She exits, schlepping that miniature carriage of hope onward.

145

MID *Heart* WEST *Land*

I'm from shit-on-a-shingle and classic prep Kraft Mac and Cheese. From the split level tuck-under, two-car-garage houses of the urban MID *Heart* WEST *Land.* I am from a weeping willow tree, Bugeaters and fields of dreams and oats—long stretches of interstate, watching the thin line run long. From the original *Footloose.* There's not a lot that separates me from green bean casserole, black vinyl, Vonnegut's *Welcome to the Monkey House,* Dylan concerts and you. I'm an only child who complained about dusting the furniture or having to pick up my room. From dirt floor basements, Brandenburg and Reese—no comments left behind. From deep freezers full of crappie, catfish and starched shirts. From talking too loud and interrupting—everyone fighting for the imaginary open mic, sharing their unfortunate jokes; to marrying into a farm family where they call me "bucket calf"; where I've learned to listen closely and butcher my own beef. From, *Go back to bed! Everything will pass.* Console television, Atari and party lines. From a Lutheran church and a confirmation pastor who said, *Maybe, speaking for God isn't my thing.* I'm from Iowa, Nebraska, South Dakota, dirt pasture. 95 percent of this region is soybeans, sows, silos—corn, grain bins and cows. I'm from miles apart—Hawkeyes and Huskers—strict borders—German and Welsh—from grilled cheese, hocks of ham and dry turkey with gravy. Here in this small city we receive texts that read: *The Yankton Police Department just notified the school district that 60 head of cattle are loose within the city limits. Parents and students should use caution when walking and driving to school today.* Where I live people say *Ope.* Will ask, *is everything okay?* If you happen to look down and out. I'm from, *Come, Boss.* I'm from watching men I admire climb the corporate ladder of American greed and discover chasing paper maybe isn't what it's all about. From Hot Wheels and Family Feud. I grew up in a Sixteen Candles generation—Aqua Net, Z Cavaricci, motley crews, skateboards, skin and bone. Where I'm from you're always welcome to sing out of tune.

Two Janitors Straight Outta Retirement

Is that trouble I hear? coming from the janitor out in the hall wiping down the wood trim around my door. His buddy, the other janitor straight outta retirement, parks the mini Zamboni outside my office. Both of them in their blue short-sleeve work-shirts with cursive names over their hearts. One old guy flips his dust rag at the other, an old-school wet towel fight—locker room style. One comes in and sprays me and my desk with disinfectant as I try to gather my papers before he gets them all wet. *Ope,* he says, *sorry about that. I hope you don't have to re-grade those.* He keeps spraying that pink liquid in his see-through bottle and moves to the doorknob of my office, the seat in front of my desk. *Just trying to get as much as we can. Everything people touch. Protocol. Which, I guess, is everything. Not sure this will prevent the COVID, but they can't say we didn't try.* He smiles. Goes to take a break on a chair outside my office. *Bread pudding for dinner today. Oh, yeah,* the guy atop the Zamboni says. *Bread Pudding. God I love that stuff.* Both sit for a spell, which, for men their age who haven't thrown in their cards and are still working, lasts about thirty seconds. *Well, I spose, we better get back at it,* one says to the other, and they giddy-up and are on their way.

Pepsi Challenge

Sixteen years old and a flop of bleach-blonde hair, some country club in Omaha, no idea who the bride and groom are and no wheels to leave, you sit there with the crush of your life at the time who's seventeen, drives a Chevette and goes to a private all-girl high school. She's wearing a tight white skirt and a dark tan. She has always seemed so mature. *All dressed up and no one to blow,* her classmate sitting at the table says. No one responds. Someone's cousin or someone's sister who's in college brings the table a round of rum and cokes and you all dive in. Soon, there's another tray of drinks from another acquaintance you've never seen and you begin to feel the buzz—the blur of adulthood you are all aching for. Fingers, hands and tongues search an endless wonder lust. All of this interrupted by the waitress who demands everyone's cups. *It's a Pepsi Challenge, bitch,* the classmate says, and you laugh and gulp yours down before you wander to the dance floor unashamed to shake, sweat and grind.

Later at the same table, with another magical round, the waitress barrels over and threatens to have all of you kicked out. That's when you take notice—she's not all that much older than you. Laugh, realize she's already stuck in this dead ass job. You, on the other hand, have your whole life ahead of you and this particular night, this little speck you've been granted, will be forgotten in the whirlwind. You will move on without the crush, without the crassness, and you all seem to know it, too, by the way you each stagger out to the parking lot and attempt to climb into the backseat, refusing to drive. Someone's looking through the rearview mirror—but who?

Faith Is

Leonard Cohen's Hallelujah played at the front of church
by this 12-year-old with a little sleep in his eyes,
violin cradled under his chin
an extension so natural and beautiful
your own hands start to sweat.
You've heard this song before,
and this kid in a checkered polo and khakis,
hair parted on the side, looks a lot like
someone you once were.
His hand glides up and down the fret board
inimitably yet so ordinarily
it silences your insistent questioning.
You need to say to him, *Thanks for holding on to
that last note. For this deliverance from doubt.*

Printed in the USA
CPSIA information can be obtained
at www.ICGtesting.com
JSHW022313300823
47592JS00005B/19